T0353186

AMANDA WHITTINGTON

Amanda Whittington is one of the most performed playwrights in
the UK. She has written more than thirty original plays for theatre
and audio drama, including *Be My Baby*, *The Thrill of Love*, *Kiss
Me Quickstep*, *Mighty Atoms*, *Atalanta Forever*, *Amateur Girl*,
Ladies' Day and *Ladies Down Under*. Amanda wrote the book for
Fisherman's Friends: The Musical. Her work for BBC Radio 4
includes the award-winning series *D for Dexter*, *The Nine Days
Queen*, *The Dock Nuremberg* and *The Archers*.

Amanda Whittington

LADIES UNLEASHED

NICK HERN BOOKS
London
www.nickhernbooks.co.uk

A Nick Hern Book

Ladies Unleashed first published in Great Britain as a paperback original in 2022 by Nick Hern Books Limited, The Glasshouse, 49a Goldhawk Road, London W12 8QP

Ladies Unleashed copyright © 2022 Amanda Whittington

Amanda Whittington has asserted her right to be identified as the author of this work

Artwork by Hull Truck Theatre

Designed and typeset by Nick Hern Books, London
Printed in the UK by Mimeo Ltd, Huntingdon, Cambridgeshire PE29 6XX

A CIP catalogue record for this book is available from the British Library

ISBN 978 1 83904 130 3

Ladies Unleashed was first performed at Hull Truck Theatre on 29 September 2022. The cast was as follows:

PEARL	Fenella Norman
JAN	Allison Saxton
SHELLEY	Gemma Oaten
LINDA	Sara Beharrell
MABEL	Martha Godber
DAISY	Nell Baker

Director	Mark Babych
Set and Costume Designer	Caitlin Mawhinney
Lighting Designer	Jessie Addinall
Composer and Sound Designer	Sonum Batra
Projection Designer	Ed Grimoldby
Movement Director	Freddie Garland
Casting Director	Liv Barr
Casting Assistant	Francesca Tennant
Producer	Adam Pownall
Production Manager	Sarah Barton
Trainee Producer	Zoe Walker
Company Stage Manager	Jasmin Davies
Deputy Stage Manager	Georgia Darcey
Assistant Stage Manager	Rebecca Maguire
Wardrobe Supervisor	Laura O'Connor
Wardrobe Assistant	Kathryn Walker
Master Carpenter	Chris Bewers
Carpenter	Daniel Lewis
Scenic Art	Sarah Feasey, Ian Hinley

Characters

PEARL
JAN
SHELLEY   } *former workmates, now friends*
LINDA
MABEL, *a Herring Girl*
DAISY, *a Herring Girl*
ALI, *a student*
FRANKIE, *a working mother*

The play is set in Hull, York and the Holy Island of Lindisfarne, September 2022 and 1895.

Time and space is fluid. The two worlds coexist, the past and present merging into one emotional truth.

ACT ONE

1.

*July 2022. Paragon Station, Hull. Platform Three. Friday,
9.23 a.m. PEARL is on her phone as an automated
announcement* (ANN 1) *plays.*

ANN 1. *The next train to arrive on Platform Three is the
delayed oh-eight-fifty a.m. Northern Trains service to York.*

PEARL. Mick, it's me. Pick up if you're there.

ANN 1. *Calling at Brough, Gilberdyke, Howden, Wressle,
Selby, Sherburn-in-Elmet and Church Fenton.*

PEARL. Are you there?

ANN 1. *And due to arrive in York at ten-oh-two.*

PEARL. It's just to say there's a chilli in freezer to do you two
days.

ANN 1. *If you see something that doesn't look right, speak to
staff or text the British Transport Police on six-one-oh-one-
six.*

PEARL. I meant to tell you this morning but anyway... I hope
you're alright. Or as good as you can be, given our...

ANN 1. *See it – say it – sort it.*

PEARL (*snaps at the announcer*). What, just like that?

ALI *looks up from her book as* PEARL *ends the call.*

Sort the roadworks you're sat in for twenty-five minutes?
The parking machine they've replaced wi' a phone line that's
dead. The app you try to download, don't ask.

ALI. I got stuck on the Number Twelve bus.

PEARL. If it weren't for the young lad in queue and the kindness o' strangers…

ALI. Tennessee Williams.

PEARL. I didn't gerr 'is name but Hull Trains should give him a medal.

ALI. Oh, well…

ALI *momentarily returns to her book:* Christina Rossetti: The Complete Poems.

PEARL. I told him we're off to a wedding. Or meant to be. If the one gerrin married turns up.

ALI. Oh dear.

PEARL. It's norra traditional wedding. They're doing it their way, you can now, can't yer? Wear what you want to, write your own vows.

ALI. So I'm told.

PEARL. You married?

ALI. No.

PEARL. Y'do right, luv. Wait till you're good an' ready. Cos trains don't go backwards, y'know what I'm saying? Be certain you're on the right track.

ALI. I'm more concerned with my studies than… I'm on my way to an interview. Postgrad at York: Victorian Literature.

PEARL. *Pride and Prejudice*?

ALI. Well, that's Regency but… Life Writing, Personal Narrative, that's my… Christina Rossetti? (*Gestures to book.*) Poet. I'm gonna talk about her.

PEARL. Go on, then. Talk. Gerra bit of practice in while we wait.

ALI (*reluctantly*). *Goblin Market*. A weird allegorical fairytale about, like, female sexuality.

PEARL. It's 'like' or it is?

ALI. It is. Rossetti worked in a house for 'fallen women' as they were called then.

PEARL. Ladies of the Night.

ALI. Two sisters: temptation, transgression, redemption.

Societal expectations of women's behaviour. Et cetera.

PEARL. Will you read it out loud?

ALI. Probably not but –

PEARL. Now, I mean.

I love a bit of poetry.

ALI. It's fourteen pages.

PEARL. Go on.

ALI. The stars rise, the moon bends her arc,
Each glowworm winks her spark

As ALI *reads, a young Victorian woman* (MABEL) *walks purposefully through and away. She carries a suitcase and knows exactly where she's heading.*

Let us get home before the night grows dark;
For clouds may gather
Though this is summer weather,
Put out the lights and drench us through;
Then if we lost our way, what should we do?

Enter JAN*, pushing past* ALI *with takeaway bags and cups.*

JAN. Coming through!

PEARL. Careful!

ALI. Sorry.

PEARL (*to* ALI). Not you.

JAN. Trip hazards all over. Hot beverages!

PEARL (*nod to the bags*). And the rest, blimey!

JAN. It's breakfast.

PEARL. I've had it.

JAN. Brunch, then.

PEARL. For the whole carriage?

JAN. If I don't eat at regular intervals, my –

PEARL. Blood sugar falls, we know.

JAN. It doesn't fall, Pearl. It plummets.

PEARL. That little lot on prescription, then?

JAN. Don't be facetious.

PEARL. Now there's a poetic word.

JAN. All I've had today is All Bran and a banana. How's that going to gerrus to Lindisfarne Island.

PEARL. Holy Island.

JAN. That's what I said.

PEARL It's Lindisfarne or Holy Island. Not both.

JAN. I'm aware of that. Like Hull.

PEARL. It's nothing like –

JAN. Kingston-upon-Hull. Though why we ended up 'Ull and not Kingston…

PEARL (*to* ALI). You're clever, why?

ALI. I'm really not. But it's from King's Town, I think.

PEARL. See?

JAN. 'Yes, I'm from Kingston. Originally King's Town.' Wouldn't you rather say that?

PEARL. Hyacinth Bucket.

JAN. Breakfast Tea.

   JAN *hands* PEARL *a cup.*

PEARL. Chai Latte, I told yer.

JAN. Five pounds nineteen. (*Nods to tea.*) Two pounds forty-five.

ALI. Is it an actual place, then?

JAN. Starbucks?

ALI. Holy Island?

JAN. Turn right at Hogwarts for Middle Earth.

PEARL. Twenty minutes off the A1 at Berwick-upon-Tweed. Train? Hull to York – York to Berwick – taxi.

ALI. Do you have to be a Christian to go?

PEARL. Let's hope not for Jan's sake.

JAN. What's that supposed to mean?

PEARL. It were a place of ancient pilgrimage. And still quicker to get there on foot.

JAN. Speaking of dragging your heels, where's Linda?

The bride. If she is the bride.

PEARL. Jan, I've told you 'bout comments like that.

JAN. What?

PEARL. She'll have got chatting to someone, that's all. Or gone to the ladies'.

JAN. So to speak.

PEARL. That!

JAN. I'm just saying –

PEARL. Well, don't.

JAN. Oh, so now I'm cancelled at nine in the morning?

PEARL. So long as the train in't, ey?

Enter LINDA, *weighed down by a giant rucksack.*

LINDA. I'm here!

JAN. At last.

LINDA. Whar a stroke o' luck it's late.

PEARL. Not if you've got a connection.

ALI. Or an interview.

LINDA *spies* JAN*'s hot beverages*.

LINDA. Coffee?

JAN. Tea.

LINDA. Peppermint?

JAN. Builder's.

JAN *puts a takeaway cup in* LINDA*'s hand*.

LINDA. So –

PEARL. Don't tell us. You miss the bus.

JAN. The next one breaks down.

PEARL. The one after that takes a wrong turn and ends up on a ferry to Rotterdam.

LINDA. Imagine.

PEARL (*to* ALI). Meet Alice in Blunderland.

LINDA. Who plugs her phone in last night but dun't switch the switch on the wall. I wake up, it's dead as a dodo. Think 'S'alright, I'll charge it on train' but me ticketless tickets are on it.

JAN. Why didn't you print 'em?

LINDA. They wouldn't be ticketless then. I charge it to five per cent, run for the bus wi' this on me back. Gerron the next 'un, jump off at the station, pull out me phone…

PEARL. Pause for effect.

LINDA. The ticket won't scan cos the screen's gorra spiderweb crack.

JAN. I do hope you haven't paid twice.

LINDA. Didn't have to. The awesome barrier man messed with the size of the QR-wharever and bing! Open Sesame! In!

JAN. She's sesame nuts.

LINDA. An' I couldn't believe it when train were late.

PEARL. Funny, I could.

LINDA. Serendipity. Fate.

PEARL. As opposed to an overcrowded, understaffed inefficient national disaster.

JAN. Thank you, Jeremy Corbyn.

PEARL. I'm just saying –

LINDA. Maybe don't? Cos it's a moment, is this. The Start of the Journey. We're On Our Way.

ANN 1. *We apologise to passengers for the delayed oh-eight-fifty a.m. Northern Trains service to York.*

PEARL. That's us.

ANN 1. *Due to train crew availability, this train will terminate here.*

PEARL. Terminate?

JAN. We've got reservations.

LINDA. We'll just have to gerron the next 'un.

PEARL. The slow 'un. With twice the number of folks.

LINDA. We'll be fine.

JAN. We'll be stood in the vestibule, Linda. When I've bought a finger buffet.

ALI. Oh, what's the point?!

JAN. Quite!

　　ALI *picks up her bags.*

PEARL (*to* ALI). Oi, it's this way to –

ALI. Forget it.

PEARL. What's up? Ey! (*Pursuing her.*) Where y'going?

JAN. Pearl, we've not got time for –

ALI. To get a job.

PEARL. Job?

ALI. Cos I'm forty thousand in debt. Be sixty with an MA and for what?

PEARL. You'll never know if you stop now.

ALI. Of course I know. Victorian Literature? I mean, why is it relevant, who even cares?

ANN 1. *Passengers for the cancelled oh-eight-fifty a.m. Northern Trains service to York, please make your way to Platform One for the delayed oh-eight-fifty-three service to Doncaster.*

LINDA. Doncaster?

JAN. We're meant to be going direct.

LINDA. Pearl?

PEARL (*to* ALI). Now listen to me. You've got years yet to give up on yourself. Trust me, lady, now in't the time.

ALI. Now isn't the time to turn up late just to show them how useless and crap and uncommitted I am.

PEARL. Or what you've battled through to get there.

ANN 1. *The delayed oh-eight-fifty-three service to Doncaster is about to depart from Platform One.*

JAN. One!

PEARL. You're an hour late for the rest of your life. Are you gonna turn back now or gerron that train?

ANN 1. *Well? What's it to be?*

ALI *looks up, startled by the announcement. She looks back at* PEARL.

ALI. Platform One.

As PEARL, JAN *and* LINDA *make a dash for the train,* SHELLEY *crosses the space, dragging a suitcase and moving as if her life depends on it.*

2.

York Station. Platform Three. 12.45 p.m. PEARL, JAN *and* LINDA *are sat on their luggage, each with a bag from Pret.*

ANN 2. *We apologise for the delay to the twelve-thirty-two p.m. Cross Country Trains service to Glasgow.*

PEARL. As they did in Donny.

ANN 2. *This is due to a signal failure in Tamworth.*

PEARL. As opposed to overhead wires.

ANN 2. *The service is now running approximately twenty-five minutes late.*

PEARL. I shoulda driven.

JAN. *I* should.

PEARL. I don't think so.

JAN. Why?

PEARL. Cos you're the only person I know who accelerates into a corner.

JAN. Well, remind me not to run you to St Andrew's Quay just because it's a nice thing to do.

PEARL. When you'd promised us Pulse and Cocktails.

JAN. Excuse me?!

PEARL. A few gifts for the Hen Night.

LINDA. It's norran 'En Night.

JAN. It's a quiet weekend before the big day.

LINDA. Small day. Just us and us witnesses.

PEARL. Rest, relaxation and quiet contemplation, I know!

LINDA. In a luxury holiday cottage.

JAN. On an island you can't gerrof.

LINDA. You can, Jan.

JAN. It floods twice a day, the tide's twelve-foot high.

LINDA. When it's out, y'can walk it, just follow the poles in the sand.

JAN. You can't say that now, Lin. It's Polish *people*.

LINDA. The Pilgrim's Way. Wooden poles what mark the path of the ancient travellers.

PEARL. Who got there faster than us.

LINDA. D'you think that young lass made it?

PEARL. By the skin of her teeth, I should think.

LINDA. She'll be in her interview now.

JAN. English Literature, though. As I said to our Claire, 'What can you do but teach?'

LINDA. She might wanna teach.

JAN. 'Business and Finance, you'll be set up for life.' So off she went to Cambridge University –

PEARL. Cambridge? Y'never said. (*Rolls her eyes.*)

JAN. And where is she now? Johannesburg. Global Head of Corporate Affairs for an international concern.

PEARL. Wharever that means.

JAN. A six-figure salary and a social conscience.

PEARL. Oh, aye?

JAN. Sustainability. That's what it's all about now, that's the future.

LINDA. Weren't our future, the fish plant closed. After all them years trimmin' an' packin', trimmin' an'…

JAN *bites into an egg and spinach protein pot.*

PEARL. How's the egg pot?

JAN. Rubbery.

PEARL. For three pound ninety-nine. Daylight rubbery.

JAN. You can't stop progress, Linda. Or as Cher once said, turn back the hands of time.

LINDA. It's actually 'Turn Back Time'. No hands involved.

JAN. I've no choice, I'm intolerant.

PEARL. That's your age.

JAN. Gluten intolerant. Which is no laughing matter when you're in transit.

PEARL. We're not. We're stuck here till heaven knows when?

LINDA. It's safe to cross till four twenty-three.

PEARL. Then an hour and forty to Berwick.

JAN. Upon-Tweed. Which nobody shortens to Tweed.

PEARL. Jan, we've been there.

JAN. When?

PEARL. The 'upon' debate.

JAN. Well, excuse me for winning it.

LINDA. RIGHT! Quiz Time.

LINDA *pulls a notebook and two kazoos from her bag.*

I'd devised it for later but what are we waiting for, ey? The fun starts here!

PEARL. Linda –

JAN. Not now.

LINDA *clicks into game-show-presenter mode.*

LINDA. Hello, good morning and welcome to Belinda Blue's Holy Island Challenge!

JAN. Who?

LINDA. Today, Team Pearl and Team Jan go head-to-head on the Holy Island of Lindisfarne. Buzzers in mouths?

PEARL *and* JAN *put the kazoos in their mouths.* LINDA *reads the questions from her notebook.*

Round One. 'Holy Island aka Lindisfarne was first seen by Linda on *Vera.*'

JAN (*blows*). Brenda Blethyn.

LINDA. Which is not the answer cos it's not the question. 'What is the name of the specific house the actual Vera lives in?'

JAN. How do I know? I don't even watch it.

PEARL (*blows*). The Snook.

LINDA. Correct. Three points.

JAN. Three?

LINDA. Like PopMaster. 'In the opening credits, we see Vera drive down the island-crossing road known as The…?'

PEARL (*blows*). Causeway.

LINDA. Correct!

JAN. It's rigged, is this.

PEARL. I've read up, that's all.

LINDA. Pearl leads six points to nil.

JAN. I've gorra Quiz Question.

LINDA. That's norr' allowed.

JAN. If somebody breaks a leg when the tide's in, how do they get 'em to hospital?

PEARL (*blows*). Coastguard.

JAN. Heart attack? Stroke?

PEARL (*blows*). Air ambulance.

LINDA. 'Our luxury holiday cottage – Herring House – was once home to a travelling army of women and girls who followed the herring fleet down the east coast.'

PEARL. I didn't know that?

LINDA. 'From the Highlands of Scotland to the depths of Great Yarmouth, they went. Filleting fish and packing 'em in great barrels.'

PEARL. Sounds familiar.

JAN. Never mind herrings, why in't there a bridge?

LINDA. The Herring Girls.

JAN. So you're not stuck there, marooned.

LINDA. Like us, once upon a time.

PEARL. The three of us.

LINDA. Four. Wi' Shelley.

PEARL*'s mobile rings. She glances and diverts the call.*

JAN. Who's that?

LINDA. Shelley?

PEARL. Course not. It's Mick, if you must know.

JAN. Why didn't you answer?

PEARL. We're quizzing. (*Blows.*)

LINDA. Do you think she's alright? Shell. Cos I've been thinking about her, an't you?

In a parallel place and time, a weary SHELLEY *enters with her suitcase. Stops. Sits. Takes a few moments to reflect on where she's come from, where she's going and why.*

JAN. Not really.

LINDA. Wondering, y'know, where she is? What she's doing? Why she don't answer me texts?

PEARL. She's with us in spirit, I'm sure.

LINDA. She's not deceased.

JAN. Do we know that?

LINDA. She's still on WhatsApp.

JAN. What does that prove?

PEARL. She's living her best life in Oz, Lin.

LINDA. I messaged her 'bout all of this. Told her me plans, our plans but...

JAN. 'Twas ever thus.

PEARL. You know what they say? Friends come into your life for a reason, a season or a lifetime.

LINDA. An' seasons change, I know but...

JAN. A baby chick can't be kept in a cage, Lin. You've got to let her spread those wings and fly.

LINDA. I know.

JAN. Don't cling on to the past.

LINDA. I'm not.

JAN. Let her go. Fly free.

PEARL. If only we could.

JAN. An' she will come back to you one day. She will.

SHELLEY *picks up her suitcase and continues on her way.*

ANN 2. *The train now arriving at Platform Ten is the delayed twelve-thirty-two p.m. Cross Country Trains service to Glasgow.*

PEARL. That's us!

JAN. Platform what?

LINDA. Ten. Ten!

ANN 2. *Calling at Darlington, Durham, Newcastle, Alnmouth, Berwick-Upon-Tweed.*

PEARL. It's over the bridge, hurry, quick!

    PEARL, JAN *and* LINDA *leap into action.*

ANN 2. *And terminating Glasgow Central at eighteen-twelve.*

PEARL. Wrong platform!

LINDA. Berwick, three-forty. Taxi onto the island by four.

ANN 2. Let's hope and pray.

LINDA. It's Holy Island. Have faith!

3.

Holy Island. Harbour. A world within a world. In ethereal light and evening birdsong, DAISY, *a young Victorian woman, emerges in her smartest hat and coat. She carries a suitcase. She gazes in awe at the sky and the sea.*

DAISY. The Holy Island of Lindisfarne.

    Lost for a moment, she grounds herself.

    Herring House.

4.

Holy Island, Harbour. Herring House. Courtyard. 5.10 p.m.
A baggage-laden PEARL, JAN *and* LINDA *are greeted by*
a harrassed FRANKIE.

FRANKIE. Sorry, what are you doing?

PEARL. Beg your pardon?

FRANKIE. What you doing out here?

LINDA. We're on 'oliday.

FRANKIE. You're on private land.

LINDA. We're looking for keysafe, that's all.

FRANKIE. Right, I think you've come to the wrong place.

PEARL. Herring House?

FRANKIE. Yes.

PEARL. *The* Herring House?

FRANKIE. There's only one?

JAN. Well, if you're the cleaner, your attitude stinks.

FRANKIE. I'm a guest.

LINDA. We're a guest.

PEARL We've got access from four.

JAN. And you should have vacated at ten.

FRANKIE. I think there's been a misunderstanding.

PEARL. There is.

JAN. You have.

LINDA. We've booked.

FRANKIE. *We've* booked.

PEARL. For a long weekend.

FRANKIE. For a week.

LINDA/FRANKIE. From today.

PEARL. September 16th.

FRANKIE. September 16th.

JAN. This is ridiculous.

FRANKIE. I'll say.

PEARL. Do you happen to have any paperwork?

FRANKIE. Do you?

PEARL. Linda?

LINDA. I wrote the address and the code.

FRANKIE. Confirmation of booking?

LINDA. Yeh. On my phone.

LINDA *searches for her phone.*

PEARL. I'm sure we can get this resolved.

FRANKIE. Let's hope, cos the tide's coming in.

PEARL. Yes, we saw the coaches were leaving.

JAN. The chip van.

FRANKIE. The Tesco delivery driver who's just filled our freezer.

PEARL. Oh dear.

FRANKIE. Indeed.

LINDA *pulls out her phone.*

LINDA. It's dead.

JAN. Oh, Linda.

LINDA. Like I said this morning. Five per cent.

PEARL. Print everything, Linda. Always.

LINDA. I've gorra charger. (*To* FRANKIE.) Have you gorra plug?

FRANKIE. I've got three kids who are tired and hungry, so if you'll excuse me –

JAN. I'm tired and hungry.

PEARL. And we're legitimate guests.

FRANKIE. As we are.

LINDA. We've booked and paid for –

FRANKIE. Look, there's hotels on the island. Try Airbnb.

JAN. Why don't you?

FRANKIE. Because we're in and unpacked.

JAN. We're here for a wedding.

FRANKIE. Family holiday.

JAN. A special wedding.

FRANKIE. Twice-cancelled.

JAN. A gay wedding.

FRANKIE. Yours?

JAN (*turns away*). Pearl's a pensioner.

Y'need to be close to the castle. Cos of your legs.

PEARL. There's nowt wrong with my –

LINDA (*to* FRANKIE). We do the vows Lindisfarne Castle, see? Then a blessing on beach. S'all booked.

FRANKIE. Not my problem.

LINDA. But we picked this place 'specially to stay, y'know, cos of its past – our past – where we've come from and what we are now.

FRANKIE. Look, I haven't got time for your issues. I'm far too busy with mine.

JAN. I'm afraid you'll have to make time.

FRANKIE. When? How? I've a six-year-old, four-year-old twins and more bags to unpack than Gatwick sees in a day. My husband's away on business and I've got a hundred and thirty-six emails to clear before my holiday starts. When I know the office won't leave me alone because that's how it is now.

PEARL. I hope Tesco's delivered some wine, luv.

FRANKIE. And I'm here for some peace and quiet, right? Peace and quiet!

Exit FRANKIE. PEARL, JAN *and* LINDA *are left out in the cold.*

5.

Harbour. 6.20 p.m. PEARL, JAN *and* LINDA *sit on makeshift seats, eating from a takeway box of chips.*

LINDA. Nice chips.

JAN. Nice an' soggy.

PEARL. They're hot, what more d'you want?

JAN. A salad, I said.

LINDA. Who to?

JAN. The barman but nobody listens to me.

PEARL. He were fully booked, Jan. He didn't have to do us a takeout.

JAN. Reheated. Microwave written all over it.

PEARL. Can you please stop pecking our 'eads?

JAN. Me?

LINDA. Quiz Question. The hotels are full.

JAN. All two of 'em.

LINDA. Do we go back to the guesthouse?

> PEARL *puts her hand up*.

> Pearl?

PEARL. Beggars can't be choosers.

JAN. I'm not a beggar.

PEARL. Yet.

LINDA. I mean, alright, it's basic.

JAN. Insalubrious.

PEARL. Fine for a night.

JAN. Hairs in the plughole, used tissues under the bed.

PEARL. How d'you know?

LINDA. We only knocked on the door.

JAN. The aroma comes seeping out. Shake an' Vac meets dry rot.

PEARL. Jan, it's a room. An available room.

JAN. A single room.

LINDA (*sings*). There were three in the bed and the little one said 'roll over'.

JAN. Roll over, fall out.

LINDA. We could rotate it? Two in bed, one on floor?

JAN. Sticky carpets.

PEARL. Fine, I'll sleep in the bath.

JAN. Shower cubicle.

PEARL. Better than sharing wi' Snora Batty.

JAN. Linda can't help that.

PEARL. Not Linda, you!

LINDA. There's a Christian retreat up the road?

JAN. Oh, so we're seeking sanctuary now?

LINDA. Retreat, not shelter. You pay to stay.

JAN. Come to me, oh, ye weary and burdened. Credit cards welcome.

PEARL. Quiz question: What's up with you, Jan?

JAN. Answer: I left Hull an upstanding citizen. Now I'm a bag lady.

LINDA. That's how it happens. How quick you can find yourself on the streets.

PEARL. We're not on the streets.

LINDA. We technically are.

JAN. When I've got three-bedroomed house at home, bought and paid for.

PEARL. Is there a caravan site?

LINDA. Norr allowed.

PEARL. Could we camp?

JAN. Oh, the shame.

PEARL. Right, that's it. Shake and Vac Towers, it is.

PEARL *gets out her phone and makes a call.*

JAN. Claire would be mortified. Roughing it like this. She only stays in the best hotels.

LINDA. So you've said.

JAN. Or the remotest of luxury lodges. They're very big on safaris, you see.

LINDA. Shooting animals.

JAN. Wi' a camera not a gun.

PEARL. Oh, good evening. We called in earlier regarding the vacancy? Well, we've discussed our sleeping arrangements and we'd very much like to –

Beat.

It's not? Well, it was an hour ago.

Beat.

We're not an 'en party.

LINDA. We're not.

PEARL. As I said, we're up for a wedding.

LINDA. A mini-wedding.

PEARL. But we've been left high and dry.

Beat.

Three of us, yes. Not four.

Beat.

Well, whoever she is, she's not with us.

Beat.

We're not 'that kind of person'.

Beat.

I see. Thank you. Goodbye.

PEARL *ends the call.*

LINDA. That's a 'no', then.

PEARL. They don't take single-sex groups, apparently.

JAN. That's discrimination.

PEARL. Same-sex is discrimination.

JAN. Same difference.

PEARL. Especially if the party exceeds maximum occupancy.

JAN. Jargon.

PEARL. And a fourth female's been seen in the village, gobbin' off an' dressed like a harlot.

LINDA. They said that?

PEARL. That's what they implied.

JAN. Bigots.

LINDA. So what now?

JAN. Ring the police.

PEARL. For what, exactly?

JAN. We've had our accommodation stolen. We've called the company – emergency line – no response. Now we've been denied shelter as same-sex females. That's a hate crime.

PEARL. No, it's catastrophisation.

JAN. It is a catastrophe, Pearl!

The birds cry a scratchy 'ker-rick'.

LINDA. Hear that?

PEARL. Herring gulls.

LINDA. Terns. Arctic terns.

JAN. We've been thrown out the nest like cuckoos.

PEARL. Cuckoos are the thrower-outers.

LINDA. They come here to breed in the spring an' go home with the babies for winter. Across the North Atlantic and down to the coast of West Africa. 'Cross the Indian Ocean. New Zealand and four months on, finally home to Antarctica.

JAN. And your point is?

LINDA. Them baby chicks you were on about. If they fly from here to there wi'out sleep or a satnav, surely we can do one night out here?

PEARL. In the harbour?

LINDA. It's sheltered.

JAN. Sleeping rough?

LINDA. Prob'ly not actually sleeping but...

PEARL. Staying up till sunrise.

LINDA. Imagine...

JAN. And the toilet arrangements?

PEARL. Shit in a bush.

JAN. Pearl!

PEARL. Needs must, Jan. (*Pulls a toilet roll from her bag.*) From the pub.

LINDA. Be Prepared.

LINDA does a Scout's salute.

JAN. I didn't come here for this.

PEARL. Who did? That's life. You play with the hand you're dealt.

LINDA. And every so often? (*Clicks fingers, sleight-of-hand style.*) The magic card.

JAN. Magic? We need a miracle.

Silence but for the terns. From the twilight, a familiar and approaching call.

SHELLEY (*off*). Sha-la-la-la-la-la-la-la...

PEARL. What's that?

SHELLEY (*off*). Sha-la-la-la-la-la-la-la...

PEARL. Listen...

SHELLEY (*off*). Sha-la-la-la-la-la-la-la...

LINDA. It's not...

JAN. It's a mirage, a vision from stress.

SHELLEY emerges, pulling a suitcase and singing the 'sweet Marie' line from '(Is This the Way to) Amarillo'.

LINDA. Shelley?!

SHELLEY. The one and only! Where've you been?

Joyful cries. SHELLEY *is embraced by an astonished* PEARL, *a reluctant* JAN *and an overwhelmed* LINDA.

As they celebrate, a distressed DAISY *crosses their space. In pursuit is* MABEL. *Both wear overskirts, gumboots and headscarves. They speak in strong Hull accents.*

MABEL. Oi! What's up?

DAISY *quickens her pace in pursuit.*

Come 'ere, y'cough-drop!

MABEL *runs after her.*

Come back!

Exit MABEL *and* DAISY, *unseen.*

6.

Harbour. 6.30 p.m. As the night draws in, SHELLEY *is holding court.*

SHELLEY. I left on Wednesday, wor it? Who knows! Flew non-stop from Sydney–Australia, twenty-three hours. Heathrow to King's Cross, train to Burwick-on-Wharevver. Taxi to Devil's Island.

LINDA. I still can't believe it.

PEARL. Twelve thousand miles.

JAN. Without a word of warning.

SHELLEY. SURPRISE, SURPRISE!

LINDA *joins in singing the theme tune from* Surprise Surprise.

LINDA. We sang that at work, remember?

SHELLEY. To wind y'both up.

PEARL (*as Cilla Black*). A lorra-lorra-lorra years ago.

LINDA. All comes flooding back, don't it?

JAN. Like effluence.

LINDA. Twenny-three years side by side at the fish plant and now... wow!

PEARL. After radio silence for how long, Shell?

SHELLEY. Been travelling, an't I? Southeast Asia, Vietnam, Bali. All over, off-grid.

PEARL. So that's why you vanished off Facebook?

SHELLEY. I'm a free spirit, Pearl. Blowing in the wind.

JAN. When our Claire comes back from Joburg, she clearly communicates when, where and what.

SHELLEY. Blah-blah-blah.

LINDA. You gerra spreadsheet, don't yer?

JAN. An itinerary. Which helps us to plan and prepare.

SHELLEY. Well, that's why I'm here in person, in't it? Cos who the 'ell 'as an 'en do on 'Oly Island?

LINDA. It's norran 'en do.

SHELLEY. 'Tis now I'm back.

JAN. With norr even a text from the airport.

SHELLEY. On an Aussie SIM, aren't I? No signal.

PEARL. It's a girls' weekend in advance of the big day, Shell.

LINDA. Except it's a small day we're having.

SHELLEY. How small, exactly?

LINDA. Maddy's staying on the mainland wi' her best mate, coming over on the day.

SHELLEY. Who's Maddy?

JAN. The co-bride.

PEARL. They tie the knot in a nice little room at the castle up there on Sunday. Registrar, three guests each.

SHELLEY. Four.

JAN. Linda doesn't want a fuss.

SHELLEY. I've got jet-lag, what's her excuse?

PEARL. Hormonal Rage.

LINDA. Lunch at the nice hotel. Maddy an' me stay there.

PEARL. And we're at the cottage till Monday.

JAN. We had.

PEARL. We'll sort it.

SHELLEY (*to* LINDA). Married, you?

LINDA. I know.

SHELLEY. To a woman.

JAN. That's how long you've been away.

PEARL. And we're over the moon for 'em, aren't we, Jan?

JAN. She'll be much less trouble than a man.

PEARL. Wrong answer.

SHELLEY (*to* LINDA). I knew you was. From the first day I met yer. Coulda told you this twenty year back.

JAN. So why didn't yer?

SHELLEY. Cos we discover these things for ourselves, don't we, Jan? On the Journey of Life what's led us here. (*Beat.*) To a rock in the middle o' nowhere.

LINDA. Or the centre o' universe, who knows?

PEARL. Either way, we've made it. We're here together again. To give Linda the weekend she wants and deserves.

SHELLEY. It's our duty, in't it?

JAN. As lifelong friends.

SHELLEY. Duty-free!

> SHELLEY *opens a bagful of alcohol: gin, vodka, tequila, rum and a bottle of champagne.*

PEARL. Oh, my Lord!

JAN. Shelley…

SHELLEY. SAY-MA-NAME-SAY-MA-NAME.

LINDA. Blimey…

> SHELLEY *sings the chorus of 'Jenny from the Block', replacing the name 'Jenny' with 'Shelley'.*

JAN. What do we drink from, the bottle?

SHELLEY. That's the spirit, Jan! And so's this.

> SHELLEY *shoves a bottle of tequila in her hand.*

JAN. Tequila?

SHELLEY. Cos life is for living, y'get me?

LINDA. I wanna keep a clear head this weekend.

JAN. And a shandy's my absolute limit.

PEARL. It's half-empty, this one.

LINDA. So's this.

SHELLEY. Tequila for breakfast, that's me. Rocket fuel to fly halfway across the world, just cos you can. To dance like Beyoncé's watching.

JAN. On Holy Island?

SHELLEY. Love Island!

PEARL. Shelley, now listen –

SHELLEY. Shoot your shot, ladies! Viiiibes!

7.

Harbour. Continuous. 'Crazy in Love' by The Puppini Sisters plays. SHELLEY *dresses* LINDA *in virgin bride accoutrements from her suitcase, which also contains various hen-night props. Bottles are passed around and the party begins.*

As the night blurs, SHELLEY, PEARL *and* LINDA *become the dancers they drunkenly imagine they are.* SHELLEY *leads a conga.* JAN *clings to her tequila, eventually taking a gulp.*

The ladies spin off and into the night, leaving their luggage and the stress of the day behind.

8.

St Cuthbert's Beach. Night. MABEL *finally catches up with a fleeing* DAISY.

MABEL. Oi!

DAISY. No!

MABEL. Got thar!

DAISY. Gerroff!

MABEL. What's up wi' yer?

DAISY. Nowt.

MABEL. So why all the fuss an' feather?

DAISY. I shouldn'ta come here. (*Catching her breath.*)

   I'm slow an' stupid and can't stand the smell.

MABEL. O' what, the fish or the girls?

DAISY. The smokehouse. You can't get yer breath half the time.

MABEL. You get used to it.

DAISY. Never.

MABEL. What d'you think you were coming to, ey?

DAISY. An' 'oly island! Norra dark 'ole with an' 'undred women who talk like 'eathens.

MABEL. You've not worked the fishings before?

DAISY. Never, no. I took care of me mother.

MABEL. Still tied to the apron strings, ey?

DAISY. Y'can't hold us here, no one can.

MABEL. Y'can't swim for shore neither, look – tide's in.

DAISY. Till morning.

MABEL. An' then?

DAISY. What's it to you?

MABEL. I might be the last 'un to see yer. Then when you drown, I'll be to blame.

DAISY. I won't. I'll wait an' I'll walk.

DAISY *pulls free*.

MABEL. All the way back to 'Ull.

DAISY. How d'you know I'm from there?

MABEL (*emphasises accent*). I 'know' cos I 'know'?

DAISY. I dun't talk like that.

MABEL. I grew up on 'Essle Road, cough-drop. Till I ran away wi' the circus.

DAISY. Y'never.

MABEL. The lass who sticks 'er 'ead in the lion's mouth? That's me.

DAISY. More like one o' the clowns.

MABEL. Cheeky.

DAISY *looks at her and almost smiles*.

DAISY. 'Essle Road.

MABEL. Born 'n' bred.

DAISY. What's yer name?

MABEL. What's yours?

Beat.

DAISY. Daisy. Daisy Dryden.

MABEL. Maggie's girl?

DAISY. Y'knew her?

MABEL. I know whar 'appened.

DAISY. It weren't what they said. She fell. (*Beat.*) She tripped an' she fell.

MABEL. Course.

Beat.

DAISY. An' I were told it were Scotch girls up 'ere not...

MABEL. A right cat's party from 'Ull? Blame Fat Polly, it's her gang. She's followed the fishings for ten years or more.

DAISY. Ten? She must be cracked.

MABEL. It's a good life for some.

DAISY. Up to your elbows in fishes' insides?

MABEL. Once you've moved up from packing to gutting.

DAISY. Bent double, hands cut 'n' cracked by gully? Stinging to blazes wi' salt from the barrels.

MABEL. Think o' the money.

DAISY. I do.

As DAISY *looks at her bloodstained hands,* MABEL *finds an old bandage in her skirt.*

MABEL. A shilling a barrel? Best crew do twenny a day.

DAISY. Not mine wi' me on board.

MABEL. You've gorra come into the speed, that's all. If you don't you're no use to no one, the boss-man included.

MABEL *expertly binds* DAISY*'s hand.*

DAISY (*winces*). Ow!

MABEL. The quicker y'work, the more y'earn. An' if you don't have to send money home – like us – y'can save it and plot your escape.

DAISY. Back to the circus.

MABEL. Bigger 'n that, Daisy Dryden.

DAISY. What d'they call you, then?

MABEL. Gigglemug when I'm 'appy, Bullyrag when I'm not.

DAISY. Your given name.

MABEL. Oh, I'm ditching that. Soon as I'm done here an' on the stage.

DAISY. Stage?

MABEL. Music hall. I can hold a tune an' I scrub up well in the limelight.

DAISY. Go on then – sing.

MABEL *sings to a music-hall tune of her own.*

MABEL.
On Hessle Road, sir, I were born,
From home and family I were torn,
Now Lindisfarne at break of dawn,
I gut the silver darlings.

DAISY. Silver darlings. Sounds nicer than plain old 'errings, don't it?

MABEL *finishes the binding.*

MABEL. How's that?

DAISY. Better.

DAISY *nods a thank-you*.

MABEL. There's nowt to go back to, y'know? If you're wanting a better life.

DAISY. I thought I'd find that 'ere.

MABEL. Me mates call us Mabel.

DAISY *looks at* MABEL *and smiles*.

You 'ave.

9.

St Cuthbert's Beach. 9.15 p.m. The disorderly group of ladies are strewn across the stony beach. LINDA is still sober. PEARL and SHELLEY are more giddy than incoherent. JAN is plastered. The kazoos are out.

LINDA. Bonus question on Anglo-Saxon Lindisfarne.

SHELLEY. Please, no.

JAN. No.

PEARL. That's enough now, Belinda.

LINDA. Aiden arrived with fifteen monks, thu'establishing Christianity in the north of England. In AD 676 or roundabouts… you listening?

PEARL. With all my ears.

LINDA. Who lived as a religious 'ermit right there, look? (*Points into the bay.*) There! On that tidal rocky outcrop named after him?

SHELLEY *blows a kazoo*.

Queens' College, Shelley?

SHELLEY. Rocky.

LINDA. Wrong. The answer is Cuthbert. Saint Cuthbert who lived on Saint Cuthbert's Island.

PEARL. With Rhubarb.

JAN. Rhubarb?

LINDA. Hence the great big cruxifix, see it?

JAN. Rhubarb and Custard.

JAN *nearly splits her sides laughing*.

PEARL. Steady on, Janitor.

SHELLEY. She's having a seizure.

PEARL. We'll have to call coastguard to get y'off.

SHELLEY. Gerr her off?

PEARL. Not what you're thinking.

LINDA. Next question! Eleven years after Cuthbert's death, what mirabulous event occurred in his burial ground?

JAN. Rhubarb!

SHELLEY (*blows kazoo*). Pass.

PEARL. That's Monstermind.

LINDA. Clue: he has passed, i.e. he's deceased. But...?

PEARL *blows her kazoo*.

Emmanuel, Pearl.

PEARL. He rose from the dead.

LINDA. Wrong. They found his body intact.

SHELLEY. In what?

JAN. Rhubarb!

LINDA. Tact.

SHELLEY. Where's that, then? Tact.

PEARL. Berwick-on-Tact?

LINDA. 'Intact' as in flesh on the bones. (*Soberly.*) Laid in the earth like a sleeping man.

SHELLEY. Breathing?

LINDA. An' THAT'S! why they made him a saint.

PEARL. As opposed to a Stephen King fling. Thing.

SHELLEY. Who?

PEARL. The supernatural horror man.

LINDA. Can we please desist wi' this?

PEARL. *Carrie*, *Misery*, *Christine*. *The Shining*.

SHELLEY. Oh my God, I love that!

PEARL. You should read the book.

SHELLEY. Them twinny girls in the hotel corridor. That rotting corpse in bath.

JAN. Custard.

LINDA. Anyway –

PEARL. There's a bit where the topiary animals cut in the hedges come to life an' attack him.

SHELLEY. Castaway island? Dead of night?

LINDA. Starter for ten!

SHELLEY (*to* LINDA). Mandy! Let's quiz you on 'er.

LINDA. Who's Mandy?

SHELLEY (*buzzes*). Your wife-to-be?

LINDA. She's not.

JAN. Maddy.

SHELLEY. Short for?

JAN. Lesbian!

PEARL. Madison!

JAN. And we're not gonna use the wife word.

PEARL. No?

LINDA. Cos historically, it's been a term of female oppression.

SHELLEY. No offence, Mrs Mick Wharevver.

PEARL. None took.

LINDA. Not to be heavy about it but –

SHELLEY. You won't take her name?

LINDA. No.

SHELLEY. Linda Square-Gardens. I see why.

PEARL. Not funny.

SHELLY. Jan's laughing.

JAN. Indigestion.

LINDA. It's about reinventing the word for some, I know that.
    Which it will. But for us – now – it just has, y'know…

JAN. Wharrever, Linda!

LINDA. Baggage.

PEARL. Mrs Michael Foster. Y'still get letters addressed to her.
    An' wonder sometimes who she is?

SHELLEY. Alright, Germaine Greer.

PEARL (*to* SHELLEY). You can talk, you're divorced.

SHELLEY. We unconsciously coupled, that's all.

LINDA. Consciously uncoupled.

SHELLEY. That's whar I said. Left the carthorse and went for
    champagne.

LINDA. Carthorse?

PEARL. Courthouse.

SHELLEY. Met, married and mullered in five years straight. No regrets *rien*, Danny Boy.

SHELLEY *focuses on an artistically placed pile of stones on the beach.*

JAN. And me! (*Dramatic pause.*) I wouldn't hose down my ex if he were on fire.

PEARL. Hose?

JAN. I'm a lady, you know wharra mean.

SHELLEY. Which ex? Joe from the fish plant?

LINDA. Claire's father.

SHELLEY. Whar happened to Joe?

LINDA. Claire didn't approve.

JAN. Claire was right. 'Be an independent woman. Go, do and be whatever you want.' I am and I do.

SHELLEY (*raises a glass*). To single ladies.

JAN. Single ladies.

MABEL *and* DAISY *run across the beach.* MABEL *dances and sings 'When I Take My Morning Promenade', made famous by Marie Lloyd.*

MABEL.
As I take my morning promenade
Quite a fashion card
On the promenade
Now I don't mind nice boys staring hard
If it satisfies their desire.

DAISY (*laughing*). Stop it!

MABEL.
Do you think my dress is a little bit –

DAISY.
Just a little bit –

MABEL/DAISY.
Not too much of it –

MABEL.
Though it shows my shape just a little bit
It's the little bit the boys admire.

MABEL *and* DAISY *whirl away as unsteady* SHELLEY
takes a pebble from the stack. JAN *falls into a drunken
slumber.*

LINDA. You shouldn't be doing that, Shelley.

SHELLEY. What, Jenga?

LINDA. They're Inukshuk. Little ones, anyway. Made by the
Inuit people.

PEARL. Eskimos?

SHELLEY. Here?!

PEARL. Not literally.

LINDA. Inuits make 'em as signposts and monuments. Great
big ones like Stonehenge.

SHELLEY. An' the 'Umber Bridge.

LINDA. No. But here, they're just summat that's sprung up,
I suppose?

PEARL. Chain reaction, in't it? A visitor sees one, they build
another.

SHELLEY. Or knock 'em down.

SHELLEY *kicks over the stones.*

LINDA. Shelley! That's strictly forbidden.

SHELLEY. By who?

LINDA. Inuits.

SHELLEY. Bring 'em on, I'm ready!

PEARL. It's more 'an a pile of stones, Shell. It's a little tiny
weeny work of art.

SHELLEY. Sorry-not-sorry.

PEARL. Meddle with an ancient custom? That's how you get cursed.

SHELLEY. Curse away!

Suddenly, thunder and a flash of lightning.

Shit!

LINDA. Blimey!

PEARL. See? See!

SHELLEY. It's lightning, that's all. Totally, yeh, it's just weather, God!

PEARL. Stormy weather.

SHELLEY (*sings*). See me dancing naked in the rain.

PEARL. No, ta. Back to the harbour, now – quick!

SHELLEY. Back to the cottage.

LINDA. Jan? Wake up, we need to find shelter.

LINDA *prods* JAN, *who wakes with a start.*

JAN. Rhubarb!

SHELLEY. The holiday cottage! What Linda sent us on WhatsApp.

LINDA *looks at* PEARL.

LINDA. Right…

PEARL. About that.

SHELLEY. Herring House. I went an' I banged on the door – BANG, BANG, BANG!

PEARL. When?

LINDA. No one answered?

SHELLEY. Somebody shouted from somewhere.

PEARL. Saying what?

SHELLEY. 'Please God, just leave us alone.'

SHELLEY *sees the look between* PEARL *and* LINDA.

So where are we actually staying? Pearl?

PEARL. Rain.

LINDA. Run!

10.

Beach. MABEL *is performing to* DAISY, *an audience of one.*

MABEL.
Fancy the girls in the prehistoric days
Had to wear a bearskin
To cover up their fair skin
Lately Salome has danced to be sure
Wearing just a row of beads
And not much more.

DAISY. You can't say that!

MABEL.
Fancy me dressing like that too
I'm sure the *Daily Mirror* man
Would want an interview.

DAISY. More like Lord Chamberlain.

MABEL.
As I take my morning promenade
Quite a fashion card
On the promenade
Now I don't mind nice boys staring hard
If it satisfies their desire.

As MABEL*'s dance becomes more suggestive –*

DAISY. Y'can't do that.

MABEL.
Do you think my dress is a little bit
Just a little bit
Not too much of it
Though it shows my shape just a little bit
It's the little bit the boys admire.

MABEL *strikes a pose*.

DAISY. Norr here.

MABEL. Says who?

DAISY. Saint Cuthbert, he were a saint.

MABEL. Oh, he won't mind a song and a dance.

DAISY. An improper song an' dance.

MABEL. What you're singing yourself, Daisy-May.

DAISY. Not now I know whar it means.

MABEL. Respectable girl, are yer?

DAISY. A Christian girl.

MABEL. Till the keelboats come in.

DAISY. It's you who winks at the cod-heads.

MABEL. Up here, I might.

DAISY. You give 'em the eye and the leg.

MABEL. What'd you have us do? Stand straight an' sing
hymns?

DAISY. Wouldn't hurt yer once in a while.

MABEL.
He who would valiant be 'gainst all disaster!

DAISY. Cough-drop.

MABEL. You're the cough-drop.

DAISY. You need reining in.

MABEL. An' you need releasing.

DAISY. From what?

MABEL. Your corset, come here!

MABEL *pounces on* DAISY, *who is laughing now.*

DAISY. Keep your hands to yourself!

MABEL. I bet it's as tight as a gnat's arse.

DAISY. Stop?

MABEL. Trussed up like a turkey at Christmas.

DAISY. Get lost!

DAISY *pushes her off.*

MABEL. You do right. Don't let none of 'em near yer. Unless you wanna be chained to the crib an' the stove for the rest of your days.

DAISY. But you've gorra get married one day.

MABEL. Says who, God?

DAISY. Whar else do you do? Follow the fishings till you're as old as Fat Polly?

MABEL. She 'ad an 'usband.

DAISY. Whar 'appened?

MABEL. She et 'im.

DAISY. Shurrup!

MABEL. She chopped 'im up in a pie.

DAISY. That's from a story.

MABEL. 'Er story.

DAISY. You live in a made-up world.

MABEL. Like 'she tripped and she fell'?

DAISY. I think I'll go back.

MABEL. To 'Ull?

DAISY. To the 'ouse.

MABEL. Why?

DAISY. I'm tired, I want me bed.

MABEL (*following*). We're pals, aren't we?

DAISY. Yeh.

MABEL. Don't pals tell truth to each other? Share secrets like I do?

DAISY. What's secret about you?

Beat.

MABEL. London.

DAISY. London?

MABEL. We work the season, you an' me. The full season, to get full wages at end. We follow the fishing right down the coast to Great Yarmouth.

DAISY. What's that?

MABEL. A seaside resort. Where folk travel to take in the air – stroll along the promenade – go to the theatres and halls. Where a girl like me can rise up the bill. Rise all the way to the Tivoli Theatre in London. Wi' you there to cook an' clean and mend me dresses. Read things an' understand 'em cos I...

DAISY. Me?

MABEL. I'll look after you, if you'll look after me? The pair of us, free as birds. Free as silver darlings.

DAISY. Till they're caught.

MABEL. Norr us, we're too clever for that.

DAISY. London...

MABEL. A new life, a better life. That's what we're here for in't it?

11.

Harbour. 10.10 p.m. As night draws in, the ladies are sobering up. PEARL *and* LINDA *hunker down for warmth.* SHELLEY *paces.* JAN *studies a website on her mobile.*

JAN. 'Top-ten Outdoor Survival Tips.

One: A survival situation is not the time to panic.'

PEARL. I think we might be lucky, Lin?

SHELLEY. Lucky?

PEARL. The storm's over Bamburgh and if it goes east.

LINDA. We stay dry.

SHELLEY. Cold and dry.

JAN. 'You are most likely to survive with a positive and proactive attitude.'

LINDA. We did weather-watching at primary school.

JAN. 'Form a plan.'

LINDA. Rain gauge, thermometer, windsock.

PEARL. Sock?

JAN. 'Identify your resources.'

LINDA. Norran actual sock. Like a cone-shaped flag what you fly.

JAN. 'Two: Critical tasks.'

SHELLEY. Critical tasks? Here's one. Grow a pair.

PEARL. Meaning?

SHELLEY. Some silly cow says she's booked your holiday home and you believe her?

JAN. 'Water, shelter, warmth.'

SHELLEY. Word-on-word, that's all it is.

PEARL. Possession's nine-tenths of the law.

SHELLEY. Where's the evidence? The hard evidence.

PEARL. Tell you what? Let's nip up to The Snook an' ask Vera.

SHELLEY. Or kick the door down an' boot 'em all out.

LINDA. In them shoes?

JAN. 'Determination.'

PEARL. There's nowt we can do now till morning.

SHELLEY. Except take no for an answer. Which I never have an' never will.

JAN. 'Recognise feelings are not facts. Focus on the tasks to be accomplished.'

PEARL. That's what we're doing.

JAN. It's vital information, is this.

SHELLEY. An' I've heard enough.

SHELLEY *goes to leave.*

PEARL. Shelley!

SHELLEY. Someone has to go back an' tell her what's what.

LINDA. It's nearly midnight.

PEARL. She's got kids in there.

SHELLEY. Prove it.

LINDA. You'll gerrus arrested.

SHELLEY. By who? There's no police on the island.

LINDA. No Vera.

SHELLEY. It's every man for himself.

PEARL. We're not men, though, are we?

SHELLEY. Who cares? We're Going In.

PEARL. No, we're not.

SHELLEY. Don't tell me what to do.

PEARL. Don't tell us.

LINDA. DON'T! Please don't. We've gorra stick together if we're gonna get through this. We've gorra.

As SHELLEY *retreats, a tense silence falls.*

JAN. 'Build an effective shelter.'

PEARL. You're not helping, Jan.

JAN. Fine. If you're happy to get hypothermia out here.

SHELLEY. An' 'n case you an't noticed, there's boats in the water. Fishing boats. The men'll be down at four in the morning, what then?

PEARL. We calmly explain why we're here. In the meantime, we layer us clothes. Huddle up close if we have to. Sing a few campfire songs an' before we know it, sunrise. Six hours, that's all. Six hours of your life.

SHELLEY. Kumbay-bloody-ya.

JAN. Do you think we should fashion a spear?

LINDA (*sings*).
    Eternal Father, strong to save,
    Whose arm has bound the restless wave,
    Who bids the mighty ocean deep –

PEARL *joins in the song.*

    Its own appointed limits keep,
    Oh hear us when we cry to Thee
    For those in peril on the sea.

PEARL. Except we're not in peril.

LINDA. I know. I forgot that's how it ends.

PEARL.
    She who would valiant be
    'Gainst all disaster

PEARL/JAN.
    Let her in constancy
    Follow the Master

PEARL. Or Mistress.

PEARL/JAN/LINDA. There's no discouragment
Shall make her once relent
Her first avowed intent
To be a pilgrim.

*The moon rises. In its pale light, the ladies prepare
themselves and their space for the night ahead. In their own
time and space, MABEL and DAISY see the future.*

MABEL. See, I'm not just an 'Erring Girl, Daisy. An' if I don't
follow this voice what's in us, that's telling us I've been put
on this earth for a purpose – I don't mean a spiritual purpose,
though it is me spirit – if I don't follow that voice then what
am I? Who am I? Why am I here... y'hear?

12.

*Harbour. 11.05 p.m. PEARL, JAN, LINDA and SHELLEY sit
and wait for the night to pass. The silence between them is filled
by the unsettling sounds of the night.*

LINDA. What time is it now?

JAN. Ten minutes since you last asked.

LINDA. It's more 'n ten minutes.

SHELLEY. Check your frickin' phone.

LINDA. Don't swear.

SHELLEY. Frickin' isn't swearing.

LINDA. It's dead.

SHELLEY. We'll all be dead by morning.

PEARL. For the last time, we're norr in *The Wicker Man*!

SHELLEY. Four witchy women? Pagan dancing, destroying
their statues?

LINDA. It weren't like that.

SHELLEY. Try telling that to the locals. Campfire songs? We'll be chased wi' burning torches at this rate.

JAN. Our Claire climbed Kilimanjaro. Sponsored. Raised two thousand pounds for a very good cause.

LINDA. Which one?

JAN. I forget now but she's walked the Peruvian wotsit, too.

PEARL. The Inca Trail.

SHELLEY. So?

PEARL. We've been to Uluru.

JAN. Patagonia. She stayed in a village with indigenous people.

SHELLEY. How long since she's ventured to 'Ull?

LINDA. Shelley…

SHELLEY. Just saying.

JAN. In case you didn't notice, we've had a global pandemic.

SHELLEY. Lucky for her and her fabulous life.

LINDA. Jan's going out there, though, aren't yer?

JAN. Just as soon as it's safe to travel.

SHELLEY. 'Tis safe.

JAN. To sit in a metal tube for twelve hours with five hundred passengers' viral load seeping out and circulating?

SHELLEY. I did. For you lot.

JAN. You don't have the issues I do.

SHELLEY. You can say thar again.

JAN. And what d'you mean by that?

PEARL. Simmer down, Shelley.

JAN. No, I'm sorry – what?

SHELLEY. Ask your daughter. Ask Claire.

From the sea, a dissonant and melancholy wail.

LINDA. Quiet! Listen… .

MABEL *and* DAISY *hear the same sound.*

MABEL. Listen…

DAISY. Whar is it?

LINDA. The seals.

LINDA/DAISY. The singing seals.

PEARL. Well, I never.

MABEL. It's a sign, Daisy, see? It's a sign.

All but JAN *are listening to the eerie sound.*

JAN. You've not changed, have you?

SHELLEY. They're not singing.

JAN. Not one iota.

SHELLEY. They're crying.

LINDA. They're singing.

JAN. 'I love me, who do you love?'

SHELLEY. It's The Greatest Love of All, Jan.

JAN. You've no idea what love is.

The seals sing. JAN *broods.*

SHELLEY (*jumps up*). Right, come on, if we're out here, let's do it! Dive in an' swim wi' em. Swim wi' the seals. Skinny-dip!

PEARL. Stop now, Shell.

SHELLEY. Stop what? Living every day like it's me last? You of all people should get that.

PEARL. Oh?

SHELLEY. Duh – cancer survivor?

LINDA. God, no.

PEARL. I do remember.

JAN. How dare you? How dare you speak to Pearl like that?

PEARL. Jan, it's fine.

JAN. Who the hell do you think you are, ey? Turning up unannouncéd after all this time? Making reference to stuff you know nothing about. Making Linda's big night into yours.

LINDA. It's norra big night.

JAN. Swanning in like the Queen of Sheba, expecting us all to bow and scrape and be oh-so grateful you're gracing us wi' your presence.

SHELLEY (*hands on ears*). La-la-la.

JAN. Us who are actually 'them' now. 'Them' who stayed, 'them' who aren't worth a second thought now you're on t'other side of the world. 'Them' who believed in you, wanted the best for you. 'Them' who you've all but ignored for the last ten years.

SHELLEY. Who are you talking to, me or 'our Claire'? Who's actually not any more cos she left you and never looked back.

JAN *gives* SHELLEY *a slap in the face. It stops the world.*

LINDA. Jeez!

PEARL. Oh, no... no, no, no!

SHELLEY. Truth hurts, ey?

SHELLEY *grabs her stuff.*

LINDA. Shelley, wait!

SHELLEY. S'alright. I'm going. I'm gone.

SHELLEY *disappears into the night.*

PEARL. Jan –

JAN. I shouldn't have come. I should never have come.

Exit JAN, *in the opposite direction.*

LINDA. Now what?

PEARL *looks to the night sky.* DAISY *turns decisively to* MABEL.

DAISY. London.

PEARL *finds herself alone.*

PEARL. Who knows? Who the hell knows?!

The night turns black.

ACT TWO

1.

Harbour. MABEL *stands on a wooden-crate stage. She is dressed as a fisherman. The moon is her spotlight. To an accordian accompaniment, she sings 'My Old Dutch' to heckles from her workmates, played from the shadows by the ladies. At the side of the stage* DAISY *watches proudly.*

MABEL.

    I've got a pal, a regular out-an'-outer
    She's a dear good ol' gal
    An' I'll tell you all about 'er

HECKLER 1. *D'y' have to?*

MABEL.

    It's many years since fust we met,
    Her hair was then as black as jet
    It's whiter now, but she don't fret
    Not my old gal.

    A wolf-whistle from the crowd.

    We've been together now for forty years
    And it don't seem a day too much.

HECKLER 2. *Speak for y'sen!*

MABEL.

    Cos there ain't a lady living in the land
    As I'd swap for me dear old Dutch
    No, there ain't a lady living in the land
    As I'd swap for my dear old Dutch.

HECKLER 3. *Does she know you're a lass?*

MABEL. *Do y'know you're an ass?*

I calls her Sal,
Her proper name is Sarah,
And you may find a gal as you consider fairer
She ain't an angel
She can start a-jawing till it makes you smart
She's just a woman, bless 'er 'eart
Is my old gal.

HECKLER 4. *So what d'you gorrin your breeches, boy?*

MABEL. *More balls than you!*

We've been together now for forty years
And it don't seem a day too much
Cos there ain't a lady living in the land
As I'd swap for me dear old Dutch
No, there ain't a lady living in the land
As I'd swap for me dear old Dutch

Accordian solo as MABEL *dances.*

No, there ain't a lady living in the land
As I'd swap for me dear old Dutch
There ain't a lady living in the land
As I'd swap for me dear old Dutch

DAISY *leads the applause.*

2.

Harbour. Continuous. MABEL *jumps off the stage and onto the waterside.* DAISY *follows her down.*

MABEL. Did you hear 'em, Daisy? Cheerin' and callin'.

DAISY. Catcalling.

MABEL. Callin' for more.

DAISY. Fat Polly yelled 'gerroff'.

MABEL. I had 'em, you see me? I had 'em in the palm of me bloodstained 'and.

DAISY. You did.

MABEL. An' when I'm on at the Tivoli Theatre, them old crones'll be saying 'I saw her – I knew her – '

DAISY. In breeches an' braces.

MABEL. What suits us right down to the ground.

MABEL *does a cartwheel*.

DAISY. Careful!

MABEL. I'm safe as 'ouses in these, y'daft lass. You'll not get your 'and on me 'apenny.

DAISY. Vulgar.

MABEL. Why am I? They're only a big pair of bloomers.

DAISY. Tell that to fella who's lost 'em.

MABEL. Lost? I found 'em washed up on the shore from a shipwreck.

DAISY. When?

MABEL. He'd staggered out of The Crown and Anchor, passed out on the stones.

MABEL *does a comedy tumble*.

DAISY. You gonna put that in your act?

MABEL. 'Tis an act now? Of sorts?

DAISY. Looks like it.

MABEL. Honest? Tell us, Daisy. Tell us truth.

DAISY. Mother took us to the Alhambra Palace, back home. We had balcony seats. Four thousand people packed in on a good night, singing an' carrying on.

MABEL. I coulda been there. I coulda sat next to you, norr even known.

DAISY. Took us back, what you sang tonight. Took us right back.

MABEL. You're not just saying that?

DAISY. Why would I?

MABEL. You swear? You swear on the Bible?

DAISY. I do. Wi' me two fingers crossed, like you when you pray of a night.

MABEL. I believe in the Ten Commandments.

DAISY. Thou Shalt Not Show Off?

MABEL. I don't kill. I don't steal or lie 'less I have to.

DAISY. Ah, but d'you covet?

MABEL. Course I do. Why shouldn't I, too, if I'm willing to graft to gerrit? Cos nobody's gonna give us a life for 'usselves, you know that as well as I do.

DAISY. Someone might. If you married, for instance?

MABEL. Married who?

DAISY. I'm just saying…

MABEL. Well, don't. Cos I'm going out there get what's ours. No matter how many o' God's laws I break.

DAISY. Mabel!

MABEL. What? D'you think 'e listens to lasses like us?

DAISY. I've told you, don't say things like that.

MABEL. Or what? I'll be struck by lightning, stoned on beach?

DAISY. Cos someone'll hear us and send us packing. Then what?

MABEL *takes a moment*.

MABEL. See that? (*Points*.) Polaris: me guiding light.

DAISY. Polaris?

MABEL.
  But I am as constant as the Northern Star,
  Of whose true fixed and resting quality
  There is no fellow in the firmament.

DAISY. Y'what?

MABEL. Me father's one of them travelling players. 'E learned
  me that when 'e turned up once. William Shakespeare.

DAISY. What does it mean, though?

MABEL. Wherever you go an' wharever you do, some things
  are constant and fixed – forever – lightin' the way.

DAISY. The right way?

MABEL. To London Town? Season's end?

  DAISY *is looking at the North Star.*

DAISY. Fixed and forever…

MABEL. Like us. Constant an' fixed in friendship, ey?
  Daisy-May?

DAISY. Pals for life?

MABEL. We are.

DAISY. Whatever… wherever…

MABEL (*laughs*). What?

DAISY. Wharever I've done? Or do. Or don't do.

MABEL. What y'on about now?

  Beat.

DAISY. Forgive me.

MABEL. For what?

  Daisy?

DAISY. Forgive me.

  DAISY *turns and runs.*

3.

Harbour. 11.30 p.m. PEARL *and* LINDA *huddle together for shelter. As night draws in, locations become more abstract and the two eras will melt into one.*

LINDA. At least it's stopped raining.

PEARL. For now.

LINDA. Clear night. Y'can see the stars.

PEARL. Three hundred light-years away.

LINDA. Quiz Question. Whar are light-years?

PEARL. The distance light travels. 'Bout six trillion miles in an Earth year, I'm told by me ten-year-old grandson.

LINDA. Gorra telescope, has he?

PEARL. Oh, aye. And an app on his phone whar explains it all. He'd go mad for the dark skies up here.

LINDA. Life, love and the universe, ey?

PEARL. He's norr on the love bit, not yet.

LINDA. Took me a while.

PEARL. You're there now, ey?

LINDA. I look back on the last forty years... twenny years as the grown-up me, give or take... an' all the things I thought mattered...

PEARL. Meant nothing at all.

LINDA. Pretty much.

PEARL. An' a hundred – a thousand – years on, there'll be women sat right here thinking the whole world turns around them and their tiny lives. When we say and do – or don't say and don't do – it's dust in the air.

LINDA. Whar are you on?

PEARL. Matter is energy, see?

LINDA. You just said none of it matters.

PEARL. E equals MC-squared, stick with us.

LINDA. I'm trying.

PEARL. Relativity. Space, time and energy. They're all moving in different ways but they act – react – with each other. I think.

LINDA. I've heard of action-reaction.

PEARL. An' I can't explain it in words.

LINDA. After a bottle of gin.

PEARL. I just feel sometimes, we're part of summat we don't even know. But what we do know? Is it all just a trick o' the light?

LINDA. If that means Jan didn't slap Shelley, I'm in.

PEARL. I don't think it stretches that far.

Beat.

LINDA. I knew she'd come. Dunno how. But down in the pit of me stomach, I knew.

PEARL. So what do we do? What can we do?

LINDA. How did it end up like this?

PEARL. I'm sorry, Lin.

LINDA. Not your fault.

PEARL. I'll sort summat out in the morning, first light. It's safe crossing from six, we'll go to the Premier Inn.

LINDA. We've gorra find Shelley first.

PEARL. She'll be back.

LINDA. Whar if she's not? What if she's lost – scared – in danger?

PEARL. Linda, listen to me. We were workmates, the four of us. Friends, great friends back in the day. But the world turns and time passes. The person – the people – you might wanna be around changes and that's fine, that's life –

LINDA. Shelley an't changed. Norr at all.

PEARL. That's the problem.

LINDA. Not for me.

PEARL (*snaps*). Well, aren't you the lucky one?!

LINDA. Pearl?

A charged silence.

PEARL. I can't do it, Linda. I can't live like this, not no more. An' I know it's gonna cause all kinds of pain but I just can't lie and pretend...

LINDA. Are we talking Shelley or...?

LINDA. The t'other you told us about?

PEARL. And now I've told Mick.

LINDA. Whar exactly...?

PEARL. I told Mick last night.

A subdued JAN *emerges the darkness, clutching the toilet roll.*

JAN. Well, at least that's done.

LINDA. Is it?

PEARL. Good.

JAN. I found a secluded spot. Covered my tracks.

LINDA. Nice.

JAN. As Gloria Gaynor said, *I Will*... well, y'know whar I mean.

LINDA *passes* JAN *a little bottle.*

LINDA. Sanitiser?

JAN. Thank you, Linda.

JAN sanitises her hands.

It's chips on a gluten-free diet what's done it. The distressing turn of events. And The Change, of course.

LINDA. What change of course?

PEARL. *The* change.

LINDA. Of course… the change.

JAN. Short fuse. Red mist. (*Beat.*) Which doesn't excuse her accusations, her deeply insensitive words but I shouldn't have – I never have – I didn't know it was in me.

LINDA. P'raps it's out now, ey?

JAN. Perhaps it's because I stand tall as a mother? Stand proud. Worked for Claire, fought for Claire, got a working-class girl from a broken home to Cambridge University.

PEARL. It weren't broken, Jan. You divorced, that's all.

JAN. And you'd lay down your life for them, that's what it is. (*Beat.*) That's the truth. I'd have laid down my life.

In the silence, a mobile phone bursts into life. Its ringtone is 'Rasputin' by Boney M. It plays from the first line of the lyrics.

PEARL. What the hell is that?

LINDA. Boney M.

PEARL. Not the song, the…

LINDA. Phone.

JAN. I assure you that isn't my ringtone.

PEARL. Nor mine.

LINDA *scrambles to find the phone as its song blares out.*

LINDA. It's Shelley's.

JAN. It would be.

PEARL. It can't be.

LINDA. She's gone off without it.

PEARL. Australian SIM, she said.

LINDA. Into the night.

PEARL. No network, no signal.

LINDA. But clearly, there is.

JAN. Who'd be ringing at one in the morning?

PEARL. Australian time.

LINDA. She might be calling herself.

JAN. How?

PEARL. Why would she?

LINDA. She might be in trouble.

JAN spots something glowing, just out of sight. She picks up the iPhone.

JAN. Gorrit!

As she does, the call cuts out.

PEARL. What d'you do there?

LINDA. What's it say?

JAN. Missed call.

PEARL. From?

JAN *(looks)*. Sammy.

LINDA. Sammy what, Sammy who?

JAN. How do I know?

PEARL. Call 'em back.

JAN. Passcode?

PEARL. All the noughts? Date of birth?

LINDA. Don't go guessing, you'll lock us out.

PEARL. So what else do we do?

LINDA. Summat's not right… summat's wrong.

JAN. Everything's wrong.

LINDA. Jan, sit tight with the mobile. Pearl, come wi' me.

PEARL. Linda –

LINDA. Now!

Exit LINDA, *followed by* PEARL. *Alone now,* JAN *tries to settle but she can't. She comes to a decision.*

JAN. The truth...

JAN *finds Linda's quiz notebook, tears out a page, takes a pen. Sits. Gathers her thoughts. Starts to write.*

Dear Claire.

4.

Churchyard. Dead of night. In the shadow of the church, a breathless DAISY *stops. Says a prayer to steady herself.*

DAISY. Almighty and most merciful Father, we have strayed from Thy ways like lost sheep – followed too much the devices and desires of our own hearts – offended against Thy holy laws.

Breathes hard.

Oh Lord have mercy – spare thou which confess their faults and are penitent – Grant we may hereafter live a godly, righteous and sober life...

As she prays, MABEL *comes upon her. Watches. Listens.*

Godly and righteous.

Breathes.

Righteous.

MABEL (*sings*).
  Wharra friend we have in Jesus
  All our sins and griefs to bear
  Wharra priviledge to –

DAISY. Go back t' Herring House, Mabel.

MABEL. We did sing us 'ymns, back 'ome. Said us prayers.

DAISY. Please –

MABEL. Kept faithful to Ma's evangelical mission.

DAISY. Go back to the 'ouse.

MABEL. The Adventists. She starts off preaching to sailors in dock. Then we go knockin'. Telling 'alf of 'Ull of the Second Coming. Gerrin doors slammed in our faces and spat on. An' then she finds out I'm singing me devil songs for pennies in pubs to get the 'ell out. Which makes us a dollymop – a mutton – a girl of ill-repute.

DAISY. Was yer?

MABEL. A evil sinner. Cast out.

DAISY. A mutton?

Beat.

MABEL. We've all done things whar abase us, Daisy. It don't mean that's what we are.

DAISY. But some things, they can't be undone.

MABEL. Says who?

DAISY *pulls a shilling from her pocket and gives it to* MABEL.

DAISY. 'Ere.

MABEL. A shilling?

DAISY. For sheet music an' I dunno – fancy shoes.

MABEL. Where's it from?

DAISY. Me.

MABEL. An 'ole shilling? Where'd you gerrit?

DAISY. Me skirt-lining.

MABEL. Who from?

DAISY. Me savings.

MABEL *tries to grab* DAISY *but she evades her.*

MABEL. Who, Daisy?

DAISY. Don't.

MABEL. Tell us who gave you a shilling?

Beat.

DAISY. Mister Frost.

MABEL. Frost?

DAISY. He drives the 'orse and cart, brings the baskets from the 'arbour to –

MABEL. I know who he is. Whar is he to you?

DAISY. Just a man.

MABEL. A man twice your age.

DAISY. Who talked to us. Which were more 'n the girls did before I… before I knew you.

Beat.

MABEL. An' what did he say t'you, pal?

DAISY. Not much. This an' that. Then 'e asked us one night to meet 'im up 'ere in the churchyard.

MABEL. An' did yer?

DAISY. He showed us his wife's resting place. Asked if I might hold his hand. It felt warm and nice an' I started saying about…

MABEL. What?

DAISY. How Mother went out at midnight. How she didn't fall. She jumped.

MABEL. I see.

DAISY. How she couldn't do it no more, see? The 'unger, the cold. How I... But anyway, that's what I said. An' he listened.

MABEL. Then what?

DAISY. He walks us back to the smokehouse. Gives us a shilling. Says he were sorry, I says it's alright. I keep walking – then running – an' then I run into you.

MABEL. That night...

DAISY. I thought it were done. That things'd be different but...

MABEL *reads her mind.*

MABEL. You're in pudding club.

DAISY *confirms it with a look and a nod.*

Does he know?

What's he said?

DAISY. We're to be married on Monday.

MABEL. Married.

DAISY. What choice have I got?

MABEL *tries to take in the news.*

MABEL. What d'you call 'im now?

DAISY. Albert.

MABEL. 'As 'e told you 'ow old 'e is?

DAISY. Thirty-four.

MABEL. You're nineteen.

DAISY. Second chance, he says. A child at his time of life is a blessing.

MABEL. Not for you.

DAISY. How do you know?

MABEL. I know you.

DAISY. P'raps you don't know everything.

MABEL. Clearly not. (*Stung*.) No.

DAISY. It's an 'ouse. An 'ome. An 'usband who says he'll take care of us. Speaks nice to us. Sings.

MABEL. Anyone can sing.

DAISY (*sings*).
There is a flower within my heart
Daisy, Daisy
Planted one day by a glancing dart
Planted by Daisy Bell

MABEL. Who'll be buried 'ere. Buried alive.

DAISY.
Whether she loves me or loves me not
Sometimes it's hard to tell
Yet I am longing to share the lot
With beautiful Daisy –

MABEL. We'll find a woman. A woman to help yer, to sort it.

DAISY. Mabel –

MABEL. There's bound to be one here among us. Fat Polly'll know.

DAISY. No!

MABEL. You want it? You want this?

DAISY. It's a life, Mabel. The best chance I've got for a life.

MABEL. An' London?

DAISY. That's yours. (*Beat*.) That's yours.

MABEL *turns and runs*.

5.

Churchyard. Midnight. SHELLEY *hides in the darkness, singing her version of 'Shelley from the Block' to comfort and reassure herself. As she sings, she catches sight of something in the shadows. Out of the black comes* MABEL, *running like a cyclone into* SHELLEY.

SHELLEY. What the 'ell, Jesus!

    MABEL *looks at* SHELLEY *like a feral animal.*

MABEL. She's in trouble.

    Me friend.

    Can you 'elp 'er?

    Can yer?

    SHELLEY *gives* MABEL *the once-over. Takes in her clothes, her boots, the bloodstained bandages.*

SHELLEY. No…

    Spooked, MABEL *darts back into the night.*

    No-no-no-no-no-no-no!

6.

Beach. 12.15 a.m. PEARL *is reading 'Goblin Market' from her phone.*

PEARL.
    The stars rise, the moon bends her arc,
    Each glowworm winks her spark,
    Let us get home before the night grows dark –

    LINDA *approaches, calling into the darkness.*

LINDA. Shelley? I know you're out there.

PEARL.
> For clouds may gather
> Though this is summer weather,
> Put out the lights and drench us through;

LINDA. You're norr in trouble.

PEARL.
> Then if we lost our way what should we do?

LINDA. I just need to know you're – Shelley!

PEARL No joy?

LINDA. No, you?

PEARL. Nowt.

LINDA. I've been up to the castle and back. Round the village, twice.

PEARL. She'll be in the pub.

LINDA. At two in the morning?

PEARL. Lock-in.

LINDA. You checked?

PEARL. No.

LINDA. So where *have you* bin?

PEARL. Round and round and round in my head.

LINDA. Pearl, she could be in the water?

PEARL. She's not.

LINDA. How d'you know?

PEARL. Oh, she's got nine lives, Linda.

LINDA. She's a Missing Person.

PEARL. An' I'm not?!

Beat.

LINDA. Right – okay – so you've said to Mick what you said to me?

PEARL. I don't wanna discuss it, not now.

LINDA. Nor do I but if you're gonna go AWOL an' all –

PEARL. I'm not. (*Deep breath.*) I just need a moment. Out here, on my own, to sort out me...

LINDA. Life?

PEARL. Head! Head, alright?

The night crackles.

LINDA. Fine. You know where I am. Well, you won't cos me phone's dead, so shouldn't we stick –

PEARL. Take mine. (*Gives* LINDA *her phone.*) Call Jan if you find her or coastguard if not.

LINDA. I can't leave you here wi'out...

PEARL. I'm a grown woman, Linda. I'll survive.

As LINDA *leaves, she crosses with* DAISY.

DAISY.
We will go tandem as man and wife
Daisy, Daisy
Peddling away down the road of life
Me and my Daisy...

A tidal wave of feelings rises up in PEARL. *She lets out a primal scream. It shakes the sky and stirs the island.* JAN, LINDA *and* MABEL *hear it, too.*

PEARL. You're alright.

DAISY. Y'are, y'are.

PEARL. Or you will be.

DAISY. You will.

LINDA runs to PEARL, *as* MABEL *finds* DAISY.

LINDA. Pearl!

MABEL. Daisy!

LINDA. Talk to me.

MABEL. Tell me.

LINDA. What happened?

DAISY. What?

MABEL. D'you wanna rot 'ere for the rest of your days or come to the city wi' me?

PEARL. All my life, I've held it in. All my...

DAISY. 'A new life. A better life. That's what we're 'ere for,' you said.

LINDA *sits down with* PEARL.

LINDA. Tell me.

DAISY. An' this is the best chance I'll get.

MABEL *holds the look. Sees* DAISY *means it. Takes her hand. Unwraps the bandages.*

MABEL.
When the road's dark, we can both despise
Policemen and lamps as well
There are bright lights in the dazzling eyes
Of beautiful Daisy Bell.

7.

Harbour. 12.20 a.m. Alone, JAN *hears an echo of the song. Then the sound of footsteps approaching.*

JAN. Stay where you are. Right where you are.

I've got a spear.

SHELLEY *runs from the night.*

SHELLEY. Stick it.

JAN. Shelley…

SHELLEY. It's an 'orror show, the 'ole place.

SHELLEY *searches the camp*.

JAN. I heard summat.

SHELLEY. I'm seeing things, hearing things, imagining stuff what in't there.

JAN. I thought they'd found you.

SHELLEY. My phone. Where is it? I left it – I want it – I need it.

JAN. Australian SIM?

SHELLEY. Nine-nine-nine?

JAN. What d'you need to call that for?

SHELLEY. To get the 'ell off.

JAN. Shelley –

SHELLEY. Gonna punch me again?

JAN. It wasn't a punch.

SHELLEY. Talk to the hand, Jan-itor.

JAN. Shell-suit.

SHELLEY. Snob.

JAN. Silly…

SHELLEY. What? Come on, what?!

JAN *holds eye contact. Who will blink first?*

MABEL *kisses* DAISY*'s hands and leaves her.*

SHELLEY*'s ringtone sounds. She sees* JAN *has the phone.*

Jan!

JAN. BT Mobile.

SHELLEY. Give it.

JAN *evades* SHELLEY*'s grasp.*

JAN. British Telecom. Not Tie-Me-Kangeroo-Down-dot-Com.

SHELLEY. Now!

JAN *glances at the screen.*

JAN. It's Sammy. Again.

JAN *swipes the screen, puts the call on speaker and holds it aloft. Sammy is voiced by a shadowy* MABEL.

SAMMY. Sahara?

I know you're there, Sahara.

Right, so you're playing that game, are yer?

Silly girl. Silly, silly girl.

Taking off in the night as you did with your toys.

With half of my stock on your suitcase.

SHELLEY *watches the phone like an unexploded bomb.* JAN *watches* SHELLEY.

Gin. Vodka. Rum. Tequila.

Champagne.

And the whole thing on CCTV.

Which you probably don't know we have in the house.

SHELLEY. Where in the house?

SAMMY. Fame at last, ey? Fame at last.

Sammy gives a tight little laugh. SHELLEY *is rooted to the spot.* JAN *is softening slightly.*

If we aren't for you, darlin', you could have just told us. We're not gonna keep you by force. But we'll save the footage. Security, innit? Night-night, Sahara. Sleep tight.

Sammy ends the call. JAN *lowers the phone.*

JAN. Well?

SHELLEY. Alright! Alright... I've not come twelve thousand miles, I've come an 'undred. From Scarborough, so what?

JAN. Scarborough?

SHELLEY. I live there.

JAN. Since when?

SHELLEY. Does it matter?

JAN. 'We're not gonna keep you by force.'

SHELLEY. She don't mean it.

JAN. Who is she?

SHELLEY. I work for her.

JAN. Right... doing what?

As SHELLEY *takes a breath,* MABEL *comes into the light. She watches and listens to* SHELLEY.

SHELLEY. Chopping veg in an 'otel kitchen for minimum wage, accommodation-slash-prison-cell. No ladder to climb out, I've burned it for bloody firewood. That's it –

MABEL. That's me.

SHELLEY. That's the story.

JAN. The full story?

JAN hands SHELLEY *her phone, a peace offering.*

SHELLEY. You don't wanna know.

JAN. Maybe I do?

8.

Beach. Same time.

PEARL. I'm fifteen years old. All done up and off to the Locarno. I'm out the door in me home-made dress and me mam calls, 'Remember now, if a lad asks yer to dance, it's rude to refuse.' So, when this lanky youth who weren't my type – if I even had one then – when he comes over, it's 'Alright.'

DAISY. 'Alright.'

PEARL. One dance. Fifty-six years. An' I shouldn't be saying all this to you when you're just about to get wed.

LINDA. Please do.

DAISY. Please?

PEARL. I've thought it through, Lin. I've thought of nowt else. Looked at it up, down and sideways. Weighed up the cost and not just financially. Worried what it'd do to the kids, the grandkids. I've said to myself time and again 'We've come this far' and 'To start again at forty – fifty – sixty.' Then all of a sudden, you turn seventy –

DAISY. Nineteen –

LINDA. And the future is now.

DAISY. The future…

PEARL. Last night, I was packing. Eight thirty-six p.m., I remember the clock by the bed. The bus going by, the kids in the street, the Thursday-night-ness of it.

LINDA. So why then?

PEARL. I didn't mean to. Or plan to, it just…

LINDA. Why now?

PEARL (*thinks*). We're selling up, that were agreed. The house needs a new roof, the garden's too big for us now, we never did use that conservatory. Too cold in winter, too warm in summer, y'know?

LINDA. Well, no but…

PEARL. Found an agent, it's going on Rightmove on Monday.
So we're chatting 'bout what we might go to. A bungalow,
perhaps? Garden flat. He says, 'Come on, Pearl, what d'you
want?' 'A place of my own,' I goes. As a bit of a joke, so I
thought…

LINDA. But there's no such thing.

PEARL. As soon as I'd said it out loud I knew. He knew. And
before you know it, you've turned round and said it again.

LINDA. Cos the truth sets you free in the end.

PEARL. It'll not happen overnight. No. No, we'll sell up and
pack up and leave together. Shake hands, split the difference
and go our separate… An' I'm not walking out on
everything. I'll tell the kids, 'If your dad's not well or
whatever, I'll be there.'

LINDA. You'll always be there.

PEARL. And we could have ten good years left. Twenty, who
knows? I mean, look at the Queen.

LINDA. She survived way more than this.

PEARL. Fifteen years back, I were going an' then, the Big C.
He got us through that an' you think, 'Well, *that's* marriage.'
Of course it is but…

LINDA/DAISY. You've gotta be true to yourself.

LINDA. In the end, you can't be no other.

PEARL. An' it's been there for God knows how long? In the air,
the atmosphere, the space slowly expanding between us.

From the day I find myself pregnant at seventeen and me dad
said, 'Michael, you'll do the right thing.' He packs up
college, job on the docks. Wed six weeks later. Three weeks
on, I lose the baby.

LINDA. I didn't know.

PEARL. Cos you dry your eyes, you don't dwell, you gerron
  an' get pregnant again. Our Johnny an' Michael an' Ruth. Go
  from a flat to a four-bedroomed house which we buy off the
  council, not thinking we've pulled up the ladder for them
  coming after. Raise a family, keep working, stay married.

LINDA. Pearl?

PEARL. Meet a man. See him once a week in the Station Hotel.
  Love him, lose him. Keep the secret so long, you think 'Did
  it happen at all?'

LINDA. You know it did.

PEARL. But what's it all for in the end, Linda? Whar am I for?
  What's been the point of me?

DAISY. Who'll remember?

PEARL. Where does it go, all this living – this life – when your
  kids an' their kids are gone?

LINDA. We won't know till we know, Pearl.

PEARL. Where does it go?

9.

Beach. Continuous. DAISY *looks to the sky and whispers.*

DAISY. Mabel?

  MABEL *catches the whisper.*

MABEL. Daisy?

  DAISY *catches her reply.*

DAISY. Y'there?

MABEL. I am.

10.

Harbour. 12.45 p.m. Both JAN *and* MABEL *are fully attuned to* SHELLEY.

SHELLEY. I'm a grafter. Never signed on or asked for owt, I look after myself. I'll break my 'eart in a care 'ome or slog me guts out scrubbing toilets cos cleaning in't demeaning.

JAN. It's an honest day's work.

SHELLEY. But you can't do an honest day's work no more. Can't earn worrit costs yer to live.

JAN. Don't we know it?

SHELLEY. I'd blown it wi' Danny cos he wanted kids an' I can't bloody care for a cat.

JAN. How d'you know?

SHELLEY. I didn't fit in wi' his friends or me workmates. They just don't get me, y'know?

JAN. Who does?

SHELLEY. Travel the world? You dunno 'ow 'Ull y'are till you're not there no more. Bransholme, Pozition nightclub, the fish plant.

MABEL. 'Ull.

SHELLEY. It's who y'are, whether you like it or not.

JAN. Until you become someone else.

SHELLEY. But Pozition's gone like the fish plant. An' Bransholme, I'd left in a blaze o' glory. Living the dream in the Sunshine State. (*Beat*.) Till lockdown. One-bed apartment, eight flights up. An' all I could think of was 'ome.

JAN. So, how did you end up in Scarborough?

SHELLEY. Long story.

JAN. Long night.

SHELLEY. I've climbed the ladder. Gone up in the world. Can't come back to 'Ull as I was. I think 'I'll get work there wi' all them 'otels, living in.' Weren't like that. I go door to door down the seafront and into the back streets but who's taking on, the way things are? Then I finally knock on her door – Sammy. She takes us on for board an' lodgings. Cleaning, bar work, all that. An' it is clean, it's safe, it's profesionally run. Alright, she's renting out rooms by the hour but needs must in this day an' age. (*Beat*.) Till you've paid off your cards an' put summat away for the future. For a nice little place of your own one day.

JAN. Needs must?

SHELLEY. I weren't doing owt – *anything* – nasty. It were naughty but nice, in a way. Virgin Bride, Bunny Girl, Baby Whiplash.

JAN (*the penny drops*). The stuff in your suitcase...

SHELLEY. The Girlfriend Experience. 'Recreating the romance and intimacy of a real-life relationship.' For gents who want a girl in their life without having to deal with an actual girlfriend, who rings him at work, and nags him to put the bins out.

JAN. What kind of experience?

SHELLEY. Some are living at home – Mum and Dad – and there's nowhere to Netflix and chill. Others just need the practice. Or someone to talk to, we've all been there.

JAN. Shelley...

SHELLEY. What? (*Laughs*.) It's just sex, that's all.

JAN. Nothing's 'just sex'.

SHELLEY. How d'you know?

JAN. You'd be surprised.

SHELLEY. Survival, in't it? Y'do what you have to, y'do what you can.

MABEL. Till you can't.

SHELLEY. Till you can't any more. So you pack a bag at three in the morning an' run for your life.

JAN takes a long and compassionate look at SHELLEY.

JAN. Does hurt, the truth.

SHELLEY. But you can't run forever, can yer?

JAN. No.

JAN opens a letter she's written.

No.

11.

Harbour. The moon is half-full. PEARL, SHELLEY, LINDA *and* JAN *feel its pull.* MABEL *and* DAISY *sing 'Goodbye Dolly Gray' as a ballad, more plaintive than patriotic.*

MABEL/DAISY.
I have come to say goodbye, Dolly Gray
It's no use to ask me why, Dolly Gray
There's a murmur in the air, you can hear it everywhere,
It's the time to do and dare, Dolly Gray.

JAN unfolds the letter. Reads it aloud to SHELLEY.
MABEL *and* DAISY *continue to hum the song under the next.*

JAN. 'Dear Claire. It's only me. Mum. Dropping you a line as it's hard to find time for a phone call these days with your job and your house and your busy life. Which I quite understand. Cos that's what raised you to be. Independent. Successful. It's all I've ever wanted for you. That's why I did what I did to get her out of 'Ull. To give you a happy life.

Of course, you'll be happily married, too. Come October. Which'll still be warm in South Africa, though not uncomfortably warm, of course. Marcus was extremely nice on the Zoom. Handsome and charming, I know you'd expect nothing less.'

Exclamation mark.

'And I do see your point, it's a long way to come. A twelve-hour flight at my time of life. The global situation, of course. When you can set up a live-stream just for me. Given how hard I can find things, you're probably right.

But I do want to say that, in recent times, if I've somehow upset you in some way – any way – I do sincerely apologise. If I've embarrassed you ever, at all. I'm plain speaking, I know. Plain in general. Unaccustomed to people you're mixing with now. A fish out of water, perhaps?

I do understand. Though the distance between us – and not just in miles – does make me incredibly sad. Of course, I know you're not coming home. I know it's not home any more. But as I won't ever be sending this letter, I might as well tell you...

JAN *sits with her unspoken truth.*

Be happy, my beautiful girl.

Love, Mum.'

JAN *holds the letter.* SHELLEY *goes towards her. Takes it. Folds it up. Puts it away. As she looks back to* JAN, *they see each other as if for the first time. Tentatively, they put their arms around each other. Hold tight. As they do,* MABEL *and* DAISY *are reunited.*

MABEL/DAISY.

Can't you hear the sound of feet, Dolly Gray
Marching through the village street, Dolly Gray
That's the tramp of soldier's feet in their uniforms so neat
So goodbye until we meet, Dolly Gray.

12.

Beach. 2 a.m. LINDA *is on her mobile to Maddy. From the shadows,* DAISY *voices Maddy.*

LINDA. So, I'm sorry I'm calling at two in the morning – on Pearl's phone, which must have freaked you.

MADDY. It's fine.

LINDA. But it's all a bit of a –

MADDY. Nightmare?

LINDA. You could say that.

MADDY. You're surely not staying out till morning?

LINDA. No choice. It's gone two, now. We might as well hang, make a night of it.

MADDY. It's not funny.

LINDA. But if you didn't laugh, you'd jump off a cliff.

MADDY. I'll come. I'm only in Bamburgh, I'll come and get you.

LINDA. You can't. Tide's in. An' I don't want you to.

MADDY. Oh?

LINDA. We've got to see it through, now. The four of us, we need to...

DAISY. What?

MADDY. I don't know exactly but it feels like some kind of sink-or-swim thing. An' before you ask, we're not actually swimming, it's a metaphor.

MABEL. Posh!

MADDY. I am posh on the quiet.

DAISY. Funny, too.

Funny-peculiar.

MADDY. Perhaps that's why I love you?

LINDA. I love you, too.

MADDY. Well, that's just as well as we're getting married on Sunday.

LINDA *doesn't reply.*

Linda?

LINDA. How can we now? I mean…

MADDY. What?

LINDA. My clothes, my hair, my… everything.

MADDY. You could turn up in rags for all I care.

LINDA. I care! They're solemn vows we're making, I wanna at least clean me teeth.

MADDY. You do make me laugh.

LINDA. I mean it, Maddy. We're not doing this cos we can or we should or everyone else is. This is our day, our life.

MADDY. Exactly. That's all that matters, it's all I care about. You and me, the two of us. Everything else is just noise.

LINDA. Deafening noise at the moment.

MADDY. So listen. Sssshhh.

LINDA *does as she asks. The silence is humming.*

LINDA. I wish you were here.

MADDY. I am. Always.

LINDA *looks to the horizon.*

LINDA. How can it travel through time and space? A voice. Your voice and mine. How do they find one another?

MADDY. Technology, innit?

LINDA. But think? How on earth are we doing this, ey? It's supernatural, it's magical.

MADDY. 'Tis when it's you on the line.

LINDA. Can we stay on till sunrise?

MADDY. Let's watch it together.

LINDA. Forever and ever.

MADDY. Amen.

13.

Beach. The hour before the dawn. Stars are scattered across the sky. PEARL, JAN, LINDA *and* SHELLEY *are each in their own world.* MABEL *and* DAISY, *too.*

MABEL.
   On Hessle Road, sir, I was born

DAISY.
   From home and family, I was torn

PEARL, JAN, LINDA *and* SHELLEY *join the song.*

ALL.
   On Lindisfarne at break of dawn.
   We leave the silver darlings.

MABEL *and* DAISY *look to the far horizon.*

MABEL. I'll follow the fleet to Great Yarmouth. Save every penny. Work on the act as I go.

DAISY. You'll be sharp as a tack by then.

MABEL. An' I'll start there. Bottom o' bill, so what? I'll work me way up.

DAISY. To the top.

MABEL. Touring shows to begin with. Look out for me name on the posters in Berwick.

DAISY. I will.

MABEL. An' if he allows you to come...

   Beat.

DAISY. I will.

MABEL and DAISY look to the sea.

MABEL. The silver darlings: they've no idea the net an' the line are just...

DAISY. It's the way o' the world.

MABEL. Don't you wonder, though? Whar it is to sing wi' the seals? To swim free?·

DAISY. We'll never know.

MABEL. No? (*Beat.*) Cough-drop.

Slowly, almost imperceptively, the sun begins to rise.
MABEL is struck by a thought.

Shall us?

DAISY. Can us?

MABEL. We're Herring Girls. Who's to stop us?

MABEL and DAISY pull off their workclothes. Underneath,
they wear modern-day swimming gear. As they are
transformed into twenty-first-century women, PEARL walks
towards the sea's edge.

14.

Beach. Dawn. As PEARL looks out to sea, the present-day
MABEL and DAISY bowl into view.

MABEL. Hiya?

DAISY. Lovely morning.

PEARL. In't it?

DAISY. *The sunrise, d'you see it?*

MABEL. *Stunning*.

PEARL. *New dawn, new day.*

MABEL. We thought we'd be first but you've beaten us to it.

PEARL. Well, you know what they say. Early bird, worm, all that.

DAISY. Absolutely!

MABEL. Daunting though, innit?

MABEL. All this. First time.

DAISY. The fear of the unknown.

MABEL. We've been there, we know.

PEARL. Right... Know what, exactly?

MABEL. They said a new member was coming.

DAISY. Why else are you out?

MABEL. Crack of dawn in September?

PEARL. Long story.

MABEL. Oh, we've all got one of those.

DAISY. The road that led us here.

PEARL. The road to...

MABEL. Swimming. Sea swimming.

DAISY. Wild and free!

PEARL. I see...

MABEL. Mabel.

DAISY. Daisy.

There's twenty-plus now in the group.

MABEL. But we're out early.

DAISY. We need the practice.

MABEL. When high tide gets a bit rough.

DAISY. Not to mention the seaweed and jellyfish.

MABEL. And Mother Nature, of course. She keep a trick or two up her sleeve.

Laughter.

PEARL. I swim twice a week. Local pool, twenty lengths.

DAISY. Oh, you'll be fine, then.

MABEL. First time.

PEARL. I say twenty, that's if the bloke wi' the windmill arms in't blocking me lane or I've not gone an' swallowed a plaster.

MABEL. Gulp!

PEARL. You think I'm joking? You should see the state of the baths where I'm from.

DAISY. Be warned, it's Baltic out there.

MABEL. But that's what gives you the rush.

DAISY. Adrenalin.

MABEL. A pure cold-water high.

PEARL. I'd be rushing, alright. Over the hill and away.

DAISY. I think that every time. I stand at the sea's edge: toes warm, skin dry, limbs heavy as lead and that old familiar voice in my head. 'For God's sake, Daisy. You've got a job, a house, a husband, a toddler, a dog. There's a million-and-one things you should be doing.'

MABEL. Of course, what you're trying to be is all things to everyone. Doesn't work. You're there in body but not in mind and then one day...

PEARL. Your mind's walked out the door.

MABEL. Exactly!

DAISY. This brings me back to the here and now. Mind-body-soul.

MABEL. Cos you have to be *present*, y'know what I mean? When you go out there.

DAISY. To find yourself part of something bigger than you'll ever be.

MABEL. An' it bonds you. Best mates now, aren't we?

DAISY. Forever.

Beat.

MABEL (*to* PEARL). So, are you changing?

Y'bought a cozzie, a wetsuit?

DAISY. No probs if not, I've a spare in my bag.

MABEL. We'll stay in depth, steer clear of the currents.

DAISY. Tread water.

MABEL. Get you acclimatised.

DAISY. Sorry, what's your name?

PEARL. Pearl Foster.

PEARL *looks to the horizon.*

Née Gray. Now…?

MABEL. It's a big thing, I know.

PEARL. Huge.

DAISY. But believe us, so's the reward.

PEARL. Out there on my own, though…

MABEL. You're not.

DAISY. You're with us.

PEARL *looks to the horizon.* MABEL *and* DAISY *head for the sea.*

PEARL. Wild swimming. Me?

MABEL *(calls)*. Dip a toe in the water. That might be enough for today.

DAISY. An ankle, tomorrow and then, who knows?

MABEL *and* DAISY *disappear into the water.*

PEARL. Who indeed?

Alone on the shore, PEARL *comes to a decision.*

15.

Herring House. Courtyard. Sunday, 10 a.m. SHELLEY *appears, dressed as if for a society wedding. She carries a tray with a bottle of champagne and four glasses.* JAN *follows, also in a wedding outfit. Both are wearing hats.*

SHELLEY. Jan, it's the job of chief bridesmaid to make sure the alcohol flows.

JAN. But you're not chief bridesmaid.

SHELLEY. An' nor are you, matron.

JAN. Nor is anyone. It's two brides, two witnesses.

SHELLEY. One Special Guest.

JAN. Special summat.

SHELLEY. Hair, mani-pedi, make-up done.

JAN. Linda's?

SHELLEY. No, mine. An' where is she, we've drinking to do.

JAN. At ten in the morning?

SHELLEY. Er, it's a wedding?

JAN. Tradition dictates the toast comes *after* the vows.

SHELLEY. As Kool and the Gang say, it's a celebration.

JAN. I'm teetotal.

SHELLEY. A champagne celebration.

JAN. We won't let on where you got it.

SHELLEY. No need.

JAN. Just don't you get us thrown out the house for drunken debauchery. Now we're finally in.

SHELLEY. Winner-winner-chicken-dinner.

JAN. Clean sheets. Hot water.

SHELLEY. Full freezer.

JAN. Tesco ice cream and nuggets.

SHELLEY. What's wrong wi' that?

JAN. Well, at least she admitted her error. Apologised. Graciously departed.

SHELLEY. Returning September next year when she's actually booked to stay.

JAN. Well, let's hope she's found somewhere as special as this for the week.

SHELLEY (*raises a glass*). To Herring House an' all who sail in 'er.

JAN. I'll drink to that.

    JAN *and* SHELLEY *drink*.

SHELLEY. Jan…

JAN. Just to be sociable.

SHELLEY. Friday night. What y'said. At four a.m. or thereabouts. When we were cold an' hungry an' knackered an'…

JAN. Close to the end of the world.

SHELLEY Did you mean it? Cos if you didn't, don't matter. I'll not hold you to it cos I *will* be alright. That's me – rubber ball – I bounce back.

JAN. Ditto.

SHELLEY. But the fact you said it, you offered… Nice thought.

JAN. I do have them occasionally.

SHELLEY. It was, though. (*Beat*.) Nice.

JAN. I am a nice person. Most of the time. And even a stopped clock's right twice a day.

SHELLEY. Meaning?

JAN. I meant it.

SHELLEY *looks at* JAN *and almost believes her.*

SHELLEY. I'm not, like, the daughter you wish you had?

JAN. God forbid.

SHELLEY. Cos this is me, I can only be me and –

JAN. Shelley, do you want it or not?

SHELLEY. I do.

Enter PEARL*, in wedding outfit.*

PEARL. Wedding Klaxon!

SHELLEY. I do.

PEARL. Maddy and Guests Have Arrived.

JAN. Never mind them, where's Linda?

PEARL. They're on the island, heading on to the castle.

SHELLEY. Via The Crown and Anchor.

PEARL. Not everyone wants sparkling wine on their cornflakes.

SHELLEY. Dutch courage, she'll need it.

PEARL. They've brought the flowers. Buttonholes.

JAN. Cake?

PEARL. At the hotel.

JAN. Confetti?

PEARL. I've got confetti – Maddy's got rings – we're all set.

SHELLEY. There's no hymns, are there?

PEARL. No hymns.

JAN. Just hers.

PEARL. They've wrote their own vows which are lovely.

JAN. So what do we think they'll be wearing? The others.

SHELLEY. Doc Martens, Jan. Dungarees.

PEARL. There are no others here, Jan. It's all of us.

SHELLEY. And the bloody wild swimmers you've asked along.

PEARL. For drinks, that's all. To make it a party.

SHELLEY. I think you've swallowed too much sea water.

PEARL. I have an' it's done me good.

SHELLEY. You'll be swimming home at this rate.

JAN. Swimming the Channel.

PEARL. Or sailing around the world, who knows?

JAN. Can't see your Mick on a cruise.

PEARL. Going solo. Why not?

SHELLEY. Cos travel's not what it's cracked up to be.

PEARL. But what would you say if I did? Jan? What would you
say?

JAN hears a different note in PEARL*'s voice. Sees a look in
her eye. Considers her reply.*

JAN. That we have to live in the here-and-now. And there's
worse things than being alone.

SHELLEY. There's gerrin a lodger. Or being a lodger.

JAN. A lodger pays rent. You're a housecat.

SHELLEY. Miaow.

PEARL. Hang on, rewind?

JAN. Shelley's back for good?

SHELLEY. As the song says.

PEARL. Since when?

JAN. And as Claire's room's vacant...

SHELLEY. Kylie posters curling at the edge.

JAN. It's time to redecorate. And yes, it might be nice to have someone around.

SHELLEY. An' fake tan on your towels.

PEARL. Well, I never!

JAN. And I might never again but for now?

SHELLEY. Hull, I'm coming 'ome!

Enter LINDA, *dressed for her wedding day.*

LINDA. Will I do?

PEARL, JAN *and* SHELLEY *turn to* LINDA. *She is glamorous, earthy, entirely different and exactly herself.*

SHELLEY. Oh my...

PEARL. I'll say.

JAN. She's a lucky lady, Linda.

LINDA. I'm the lucky one. An' I just wanna say before it all starts that I wouldn't be here wi'out you. All of you. I'd take me 'at off to you, except it'd mess wi' me hair.

PEARL. Don't do that.

JAN. No.

SHELLEY. Never do that.

LINDA looks at her friends.

LINDA. Werra big win, weren't it? Us four, meeting up as we did on the factory floor.

PEARL. We hit the jackpot.

JAN. Been through the highs and lows.

SHELLEY. An' that were just Friday night.

LINDA. Still here though, aren't we?

PEARL. Surviving.

JAN. Family.

SHELLEY. Friends.

SHELLEY hands LUCY a full glass.

All four drain their glasses.

LINDA. Oh my God, look at the time!

A scramble of bags, shoes, lipstick and hat-adjustment.

PEARL. Ladies?

JAN. Cometh the hour.

SHELLEY. Cometh the party till dawn, why not?

PEARL. Me age.

JAN. Me gut.

LINDA. Me new wife?

SHELLEY. Me new life.

The ladies are finally set.

PEARL. Ready?

JAN/SHELLEY/LINDA. As I'll ever be.

Laughter.

PEARL. Let's do it, ladies! Let's live!

The End.

In the curtain call, the cast may unleash their spirits and lead a wedding-disco dance to 'Single Ladies (Put a Ring on It)' by Beyoncé.

www.nickhernbooks.co.uk

facebook.com/nickhernbooks

twitter.com/nickhernbooks